Mastering Quality Control: A Guide for Industrial Engineers

Clinton

Copyright © [2023]

Title: Mastering Quality Control: A Guide for Industrial Engineers
Author's: Clinton

All rights reserved. No part of this publication may be reproduced, stored in a retrieval system, or transmitted in any form or by any means, electronic, mechanical, photocopying, recording, or otherwise, without the prior written permission of the publisher or author, except in the case of brief quotations embodied in critical reviews and certain other non-commercial uses permitted by copyright law.

This book was printed and published by [Publisher's: **Clinton**] in [2023]

ISBN:

TABLE OF CONTENT

Chapter 1: Introduction to Quality Control in Industrial Engineering   08

Understanding the Importance of Quality Control

Overview of Industrial Engineering and its Role in Quality Control

Key Concepts and Terminology in Quality Control

Chapter 2: Quality Control Tools and Techniques   14

Statistical Process Control (SPC)

Control Charts

Pareto Analysis

Cause and Effect Diagrams

Failure Mode and Effects Analysis (FMEA)

Root Cause Analysis

Six Sigma Methodology

Chapter 3: Designing Effective Quality Control Systems 29

Setting Quality Objectives and Metrics

Developing Standard Operating Procedures (SOPs)

Establishing Quality Control Plans

Documenting and Communicating Quality Procedures

Implementing Quality Control Training Programs

Chapter 4: Quality Control in Manufacturing Processes 40

Defining Key Performance Indicators (KPIs) for Manufacturing

Process Mapping and Analysis

Identifying and Eliminating Waste in Manufacturing

Standardizing Work Instructions

Implementing Continuous Improvement Initiatives

Chapter 5: Quality Control in Supply Chain Management 52

Ensuring Supplier Quality

Vendor Evaluation and Performance Monitoring

Implementing Effective Supplier Audits

Managing Product Quality throughout the Supply Chain

Reducing Lead Time and Enhancing Delivery Performance

Chapter 6: Quality Control in Service Industries 62

Understanding the Unique Challenges of Service Quality Control

Developing Service Quality Standards

Conducting Service Process Audits

Implementing Quality Control in Service Delivery

Managing Customer Feedback and Complaints

Chapter 7: Quality Control and Continuous Improvement Culture 74

Fostering a Culture of Quality in Industrial Engineering

Strategies for Employee Engagement in Quality Control

Continuous Improvement Tools and Techniques

Implementing Lean Principles in Quality Control

Sustaining Quality Control Efforts in the Long Term

Chapter 8: Quality Control Case Studies 86

Case Study 1: Improving Product Quality in a Manufacturing Plant

Case Study 2: Enhancing Service Quality in a Healthcare Setting

Case Study 3: Implementing Six Sigma in a Logistics Company

Case Study 4: Overcoming Quality Challenges in a Construction Project

Chapter 9: Future Trends and Innovations in Quality Control 97

Industry 4.0 and its Impact on Quality Control

Automation and Robotics in Quality Assurance

Artificial Intelligence and Machine Learning in Quality Control

Big Data Analytics for Quality Improvement

Predictive Maintenance and Quality Control

Chapter 10: Conclusion and Final Thoughts 107

Recap of Key Concepts and Strategies

Importance of Continuous Learning and Adaptation in Quality Control

Final Words of Encouragement for Industrial Engineers on Mastering Quality Control

Chapter 1: Introduction to Quality Control in Industrial Engineering

Understanding the Importance of Quality Control

Quality control is an essential aspect of any industrial engineering process. It ensures that products and services meet the required standards and specifications, guaranteeing customer satisfaction and maintaining the reputation of a company. In this subchapter, we will delve into the significance of quality control in the field of industrial engineering and how it impacts various niches within this sector.

Quality control involves a series of systematic activities that are performed to monitor and measure the characteristics of a product or service. By implementing quality control measures, industrial engineers can identify defects, errors, and deviations from the desired standards early in the production process. This enables them to take corrective actions promptly, minimizing waste and avoiding costly rework or recalls.

In the realm of industrial engineering, quality control plays a vital role in ensuring efficient operations. It helps in streamlining processes, reducing variability, and enhancing overall productivity. By closely monitoring the quality of inputs, intermediate steps, and final outputs, industrial engineers can identify areas for improvement and implement effective measures to enhance efficiency and reduce costs.

Moreover, quality control is crucial in meeting customer expectations and maintaining a competitive edge. Customers today have become more discerning and demand products and services that consistently meet or exceed their expectations. By implementing stringent quality control measures, industrial engineers can ensure that their products and services are of high quality, leading to increased customer satisfaction and loyalty.

Different niches within the field of industrial engineering benefit from quality control in unique ways. In manufacturing, quality control helps identify and rectify issues that may arise during production, such as machine malfunctions or raw material defects. In supply chain management, quality control ensures that products meet the required specifications before they are shipped to customers. In project management, quality control helps in monitoring and controlling project activities to ensure adherence to quality standards.

In conclusion, quality control is of utmost importance in the field of industrial engineering. It not only guarantees customer satisfaction but also enhances operational efficiency, reduces costs, and maintains a competitive advantage. By understanding and implementing effective quality control measures, industrial engineers can ensure the success and growth of their organizations in a dynamic and demanding market.

Overview of Industrial Engineering and its Role in Quality Control

Industrial engineering is a field that focuses on optimizing complex systems and processes to enhance productivity, efficiency, and quality in various industries. It applies scientific principles to design, improve, and implement integrated systems of people, materials, information, equipment, and energy. One of the key areas where industrial engineering plays a crucial role is quality control.

Quality control is an essential aspect of any manufacturing or production process. It ensures that products and services meet or exceed customer expectations by adhering to specified standards and requirements. Industrial engineers are central to this process as they possess the expertise to identify and eliminate inefficiencies, optimize processes, and maintain quality standards.

Industrial engineers apply statistical analysis, mathematical modeling, and data-driven techniques to measure, monitor, and control quality throughout the production cycle. They analyze production systems, identify potential bottlenecks, and suggest improvements to enhance quality. By implementing effective quality control measures, industrial engineers ensure that defects and errors are minimized, resulting in cost savings and improved customer satisfaction.

In the context of quality control, industrial engineers employ a range of tools and methodologies such as Six Sigma, Lean Manufacturing, Total Quality Management (TQM), and Statistical Process Control (SPC). These approaches help identify variations, defects, or deviations from established standards, allowing for timely corrective actions to be taken. Industrial engineers also design and implement quality control systems, including inspection procedures, testing protocols, and quality assurance processes.

Moreover, industrial engineers play a vital role in ensuring consistent quality by conducting audits, evaluating suppliers, and monitoring production lines. They work closely with cross-functional teams to develop and implement quality improvement initiatives, train employees on quality control practices, and foster a culture of continuous improvement.

The impact of industrial engineering on quality control extends beyond manufacturing sectors. It also applies to service industries such as healthcare, logistics, and transportation, where processes need to be optimized to deliver high-quality services efficiently.

In conclusion, industrial engineering is a critical discipline that drives quality control efforts across various industries. By leveraging their expertise in system optimization, data analysis, and process improvement, industrial engineers contribute to enhancing product quality, reducing costs, and ensuring customer satisfaction. Their role in quality control is indispensable, and their efforts are invaluable in helping organizations achieve their quality objectives.

Key Concepts and Terminology in Quality Control

Quality control is an essential aspect of industrial engineering, ensuring that products and processes meet set standards and requirements. To effectively navigate the field of quality control, it is important to understand key concepts and terminology. This subchapter aims to provide a comprehensive overview of these concepts, catering to an audience of industrial engineers.

1. Quality Control: Quality control refers to the systematic approach used to maintain and improve the quality of products or services. It involves monitoring, measuring, and controlling various aspects of production processes to ensure consistency and adherence to predetermined standards.

2. Defect: A defect is a non-conformance or deviation from a specified requirement. It can manifest in various forms, such as physical flaws, functionality issues, or incorrect measurements. Identification and rectification of defects are vital to maintaining high product quality.

3. Statistical Process Control (SPC): SPC is a methodology that employs statistical tools and techniques to monitor and control production processes. It aids in identifying variations and trends, enabling engineers to make data-driven decisions and take corrective actions.

4. Six Sigma: Six Sigma is a disciplined, data-driven approach to process improvement. It aims to minimize defects and variations by employing statistical analysis and problem-solving techniques. The ultimate goal of Six Sigma is to achieve near-perfect performance, with a defect rate of 3.4 parts per million.

5. Quality Assurance (QA): Quality assurance encompasses all planned and systematic activities aimed at ensuring that products or services meet specified requirements. It includes processes like inspection, testing, and audits to identify and rectify deviations from set standards.

6. Total Quality Management (TQM): TQM is a management philosophy that focuses on continuous improvement and customer satisfaction. It emphasizes the involvement of all employees in quality-related activities and the integration of quality principles into all aspects of the organization.

7. Pareto Analysis: Pareto analysis is a technique used to prioritize problems or issues based on their impact. It follows the 80/20 rule, stating that 80% of the problems are caused by 20% of the factors. By identifying and addressing the vital few factors, engineers can effectively allocate resources and improve overall quality.

8. Control Charts: Control charts are graphical tools used to monitor processes over time. They display data points along with control limits, allowing engineers to identify when a process is out of control or exhibiting unusual variations.

By familiarizing themselves with these key concepts and terminology, industrial engineers can enhance their understanding and application of quality control principles. Mastering these concepts will enable engineers to effectively implement quality control strategies, ensuring the delivery of high-quality products and services while optimizing production processes.

Chapter 2: Quality Control Tools and Techniques

Statistical Process Control (SPC)

Statistical Process Control (SPC) is a key concept in the field of Industrial Engineering that aims to monitor and control the quality of processes in order to ensure consistent and reliable production outcomes. This subchapter of the book "Mastering Quality Control: A Guide for Industrial Engineers" provides a comprehensive overview of SPC, its principles, and its practical applications.

SPC is a data-driven approach that employs statistical techniques to analyze and evaluate the variations in a process. By collecting and analyzing data at various stages of a production process, engineers can gain insights into the sources of variation and make informed decisions to achieve desired quality levels. The ultimate goal of SPC is to identify and eliminate special causes of variation while reducing common causes to achieve a state of statistical control.

The subchapter begins by explaining the basic principles of SPC, including the concept of variation, types of variation, and the importance of understanding and controlling variation in industrial processes. It then delves into the different statistical tools and techniques used in SPC, such as control charts, process capability analysis, and acceptance sampling.

Control charts are a fundamental tool in SPC that help visualize process variation over time. The subchapter describes the different types of control charts, such as X-bar and R charts, and provides step-by-step instructions on how to construct and interpret them. It also highlights the significance of control limits, which help determine whether a process is within acceptable limits or if it requires corrective action.

Process capability analysis is another essential aspect of SPC covered in the subchapter. It explains how to assess a process's ability to consistently meet customer specifications and provides guidelines on how to interpret process capability indices, such as Cp and Cpk.

Moreover, the subchapter discusses the concept of acceptance sampling, a technique used to inspect a sample of products or materials for quality conformance. It explains different sampling plans and their applications in various scenarios.

Overall, this subchapter on Statistical Process Control (SPC) provides a comprehensive understanding of the principles and techniques used in Industrial Engineering to monitor and control process quality. It equips readers with the knowledge to implement SPC effectively, leading to improved product quality, reduced costs, and increased customer satisfaction.

Control Charts

Control charts are an essential tool in the field of industrial engineering for monitoring and improving the quality of processes. They provide a visual representation of process variation, allowing engineers to identify and address issues before they result in defects or deviations from desired specifications. This subchapter explores the fundamentals of control charts and their applications in the context of quality control.

Understanding Control Charts

Control charts are graphical representations of process data over time, enabling engineers to determine whether a process is in a state of statistical control. By plotting sample measurements or data points on a chart, engineers can analyze patterns and trends to determine if the process is functioning within acceptable limits.

There are two main types of control charts: variable control charts and attribute control charts. Variable control charts are used when the quality characteristic being measured is a continuous variable, such as weight or length. Attribute control charts, on the other hand, are used when the quality characteristic is discrete or categorical, such as the number of defects or the presence of a certain feature.

Applications of Control Charts

Control charts offer numerous benefits to industrial engineers in improving quality control processes. By monitoring process variation, control charts enable engineers to identify and eliminate special causes of variation, which are non-random factors that contribute to defects or deviations from specifications. This helps in preventing costly rework, reducing waste, and improving overall process efficiency.

Control charts also aid in detecting changes in process performance over time. By analyzing patterns on the control chart, engineers can identify shifts, trends, or cyclical variations that may indicate a need for process adjustment or improvement. This proactive approach helps prevent quality issues before they occur and ensures consistent product quality.

Furthermore, control charts provide a basis for making data-driven decisions. Engineers can set control limits based on statistical analysis, allowing them to distinguish between common cause variation (inherent to the process) and special cause variation (resulting from external factors). This enables them to take appropriate actions to maintain process stability and improve long-term performance.

In conclusion, control charts are a powerful tool for industrial engineers in mastering quality control. By visually representing process variation over time, control charts allow engineers to monitor process performance, identify special causes of variation, and make data-driven decisions. By implementing control charts effectively, engineers can enhance product quality, minimize defects, and optimize process efficiency.

Pareto Analysis

Pareto Analysis is a powerful tool that can be utilized by industrial engineers to identify and prioritize the most significant factors contributing to quality control issues. Named after the Italian economist Vilfredo Pareto, this technique is based on the Pareto principle, also known as the 80/20 rule. The principle states that roughly 80% of the effects come from 20% of the causes.

In the context of quality control, Pareto Analysis enables engineers to focus their efforts on the critical few factors that have the most significant impact on product or process quality. By identifying and addressing these key factors, industrial engineers can maximize their efficiency and improve overall quality control outcomes.

The first step in conducting a Pareto Analysis is to gather data related to the quality control issues at hand. This data can include customer complaints, defect rates, or any other relevant information. Once the data is collected, it is essential to categorize it into different groups or categories. For example, if the quality control issue is related to product defects, categories could include design flaws, manufacturing errors, or material defects.

After categorization, the data is then graphically represented in a Pareto chart, which displays the frequency or impact of each category in descending order. The chart typically consists of bars representing each category's frequency or impact, with the categories listed on the x-axis and the frequency or impact on the y-axis. The chart also includes a cumulative percentage line, showing the cumulative contribution of each category.

Analyzing the Pareto chart allows industrial engineers to identify the vital few categories that account for the majority of quality control issues. By focusing on these categories, engineers can allocate their resources effectively and address the root causes of the problems. This targeted approach helps reduce waste, improve efficiency, and enhance overall product or process quality.

Pareto Analysis is not only applicable to quality control issues but can also be used in various other industrial engineering applications. Whether it is identifying the critical few factors affecting productivity, safety incidents, or equipment failures, Pareto Analysis provides a structured and logical approach to problem-solving.

In conclusion, Pareto Analysis is a valuable tool for industrial engineers in their quest for mastering quality control. By utilizing this technique, engineers can prioritize their efforts, address the most significant issues, and achieve improved outcomes. Whether you are an industrial engineer or anyone interested in quality control, understanding and applying the principles of Pareto Analysis will undoubtedly enhance your ability to identify and solve problems efficiently.

Cause and Effect Diagrams

In the world of industrial engineering, analyzing and improving processes is a fundamental aspect to ensure quality control. One of the most effective tools used for this purpose is the Cause and Effect diagram, also known as the Ishikawa or fishbone diagram. This subchapter will delve into the intricacies of Cause and Effect diagrams, their significance, and how they can be applied to various industrial engineering processes.

Cause and Effect diagrams are visual representations that help identify the potential causes of a problem or an effect. They provide a structured approach to problem-solving by breaking down complex issues into manageable components. By visually organizing the potential causes, engineers can prioritize and tackle each factor individually, leading to more efficient and effective problem-solving.

The diagram takes its name from its appearance, resembling the skeleton of a fish, with the effect or problem of interest at the head and the potential causes branching out as bones. These branches are categorized into major categories, such as equipment, materials, methods, people, and environment, allowing for a comprehensive analysis of all possible causes.

Every industrial engineer can benefit from using Cause and Effect diagrams. They not only help identify the root cause of a problem but also enable engineers to understand the relationships between different factors. This knowledge is crucial for developing effective strategies to eliminate or mitigate the causes, leading to improved process efficiency and quality control.

Furthermore, Cause and Effect diagrams encourage teamwork and collaboration. By involving various stakeholders, such as operators, technicians, and managers, in the diagramming process, a more holistic understanding of the problem can be achieved. This collaborative effort fosters a culture of continuous improvement and empowers everyone involved to contribute their expertise and insights.

To successfully create a Cause and Effect diagram, several steps must be followed. These include defining the problem or effect, brainstorming potential causes, organizing these causes into categories, and analyzing the potential causes to identify the most likely root cause. The diagram can be developed manually using pen and paper or through specialized software, based on the engineers' preference and available resources.

In conclusion, Cause and Effect diagrams are valuable tools for industrial engineers in the pursuit of quality control. Their ability to visually represent complex problems and potential causes facilitates effective problem-solving and promotes collaboration. By incorporating Cause and Effect diagrams into their toolbox, industrial engineers can enhance their ability to analyze and optimize processes, ultimately leading to improved productivity and customer satisfaction.

Failure Mode and Effects Analysis (FMEA)

In the world of industrial engineering, ensuring the highest level of quality control is of utmost importance. One powerful tool that helps achieve this goal is Failure Mode and Effects Analysis (FMEA). FMEA is a systematic approach used to identify potential failures in a product or process, assess their impact, and prioritize actions to prevent or mitigate them.

FMEA is a valuable technique that can be applied to various stages of a product's lifecycle, from design and development to manufacturing and even after-sales service. By proactively identifying potential failure modes and their effects, industrial engineers can take necessary steps to minimize risks and enhance product reliability.

The process of conducting an FMEA involves a multidisciplinary team that includes design engineers, manufacturing specialists, quality engineers, and other stakeholders. The team collaboratively analyzes each component or process step, documenting all possible ways in which it could fail. These potential failure modes are then ranked based on their severity, occurrence probability, and detectability.

Once the failure modes are identified and ranked, the team can focus on developing effective strategies to prevent or control them. This may involve redesigning the product, implementing additional quality control measures, or improving manufacturing processes. By taking proactive measures to address potential failure modes, industrial engineers can save time, reduce costs, and enhance overall product quality.

FMEA also plays a crucial role in risk management. By identifying potential failures and their effects early on, industrial engineers can prioritize their efforts towards critical areas that have the highest impact. This allows for efficient allocation of resources and ensures that the most significant risks are effectively managed.

Industries ranging from automotive and aerospace to electronics and pharmaceuticals have widely adopted FMEA as a standard practice. It is a versatile and adaptable tool that can be customized to suit specific industry requirements and product complexities.

In conclusion, Failure Mode and Effects Analysis (FMEA) is an essential tool in the arsenal of industrial engineers. It enables them to identify potential failures, assess their impact, and develop effective strategies to prevent or mitigate them. By utilizing FMEA, industrial engineers can enhance product quality, minimize risks, and ensure customer satisfaction.

Root Cause Analysis

In the world of industrial engineering, identifying and resolving issues is a critical component of ensuring quality control. One of the most effective tools to achieve this is Root Cause Analysis (RCA). This subchapter aims to provide a comprehensive understanding of RCA and how it can be implemented to enhance quality control practices across various industries.

Root Cause Analysis is a systematic approach used to identify the underlying causes of problems and defects. It goes beyond addressing the symptoms and delves into the core issues that give rise to these challenges. By analyzing the root causes, engineers can develop effective solutions to prevent the recurrence of problems, leading to improved product quality and operational efficiency.

This subchapter will provide an overview of the RCA process, outlining the key steps involved. It will discuss the importance of gathering data and evidence, as well as the various techniques employed to identify root causes, such as the 5 Whys, Fishbone Diagrams, and Pareto Analysis.

Additionally, this subchapter will highlight the benefits of implementing RCA in industrial engineering. It will emphasize how RCA can lead to cost savings, increased customer satisfaction, and improved overall productivity. Real-world case studies will be presented to demonstrate the successful application of RCA in different industrial settings, showcasing its effectiveness in problem-solving.

Furthermore, the subchapter will address common challenges faced during RCA implementation and provide strategies to overcome them. It will emphasize the need for a multidisciplinary approach, involving the collaboration of various stakeholders, including engineers, operators, and management, to ensure the success of the RCA process.

Finally, this subchapter will explore the integration of RCA with other quality control tools and methodologies, such as Six Sigma and Lean Manufacturing. It will discuss how RCA can complement these approaches, enhancing their effectiveness in identifying and eliminating root causes of defects.

Overall, this subchapter aims to equip industrial engineers with the knowledge and skills needed to implement Root Cause Analysis effectively. By mastering this technique, engineers can play a pivotal role in improving quality control practices, reducing defects, and enhancing overall operational performance in various industries.

Six Sigma Methodology

Introduction:
In the field of Industrial Engineering, the Six Sigma methodology has emerged as a powerful quality control tool. This subchapter will provide an overview of Six Sigma, its principles, and how it can be effectively applied in different industrial engineering settings. Whether you are a novice or an experienced professional, understanding and implementing Six Sigma can significantly enhance your ability to improve quality control processes in your organization.

What is Six Sigma?
Six Sigma is a disciplined approach to quality management that aims to reduce defects, errors, and variations in manufacturing and service processes. It provides a framework for identifying, analyzing, and eliminating the root causes of process inefficiencies, thereby improving customer satisfaction and profitability. Originally developed by Motorola in the 1980s, Six Sigma has since gained popularity across various industries due to its proven results.

Key Principles of Six Sigma:
The foundation of Six Sigma is built on two key principles: process improvement and statistical analysis. By focusing on improving processes, Six Sigma helps organizations achieve consistent, predictable, and high-quality results. Statistical analysis enables practitioners to measure process performance, identify areas of improvement, and make data-driven decisions.

DMAIC Methodology:
Six Sigma follows a structured problem-solving approach known as

DMAIC (Define, Measure, Analyze, Improve, Control). This methodology guides practitioners through five phases, starting with defining the problem, measuring the current state, analyzing data, implementing improvements, and establishing control measures to sustain the improvements.

Tools and Techniques:
To effectively implement Six Sigma, industrial engineers utilize a range of tools and techniques. These include process mapping, cause-and-effect diagrams, failure mode and effects analysis (FMEA), control charts, statistical process control (SPC), and design of experiments (DOE). Each tool plays a specific role in identifying and addressing process inefficiencies.

Benefits of Six Sigma:
Implementing Six Sigma methodology offers numerous benefits to industrial engineering professionals and their organizations. It helps reduce defects and errors, optimize processes, enhance customer satisfaction, increase operational efficiency, and ultimately improve the bottom line. Moreover, Six Sigma fosters a culture of continuous improvement and empowers employees to take ownership of quality control initiatives.

Conclusion:
Six Sigma methodology is an essential tool for industrial engineers seeking to enhance quality control processes. By following the DMAIC methodology and utilizing various statistical tools, professionals can identify and eliminate process inefficiencies, resulting in improved customer satisfaction and increased profitability. Embracing Six Sigma

principles can transform organizations by fostering a culture of quality and continuous improvement.

Chapter 3: Designing Effective Quality Control Systems

Setting Quality Objectives and Metrics

In the dynamic and competitive world of industrial engineering, maintaining a high level of quality control is crucial for success. To achieve this, it is essential to set clear quality objectives and establish relevant metrics to measure and monitor progress. This subchapter will delve into the significance of setting quality objectives and metrics, providing valuable insights and guidance for industrial engineers.

Quality objectives serve as a roadmap towards achieving desired outcomes and ensuring customer satisfaction. They provide a clear direction for the organization, aligning all stakeholders towards a common purpose. By setting quality objectives, industrial engineers can define specific targets related to product or service quality, process efficiency, and customer experience. These objectives act as a yardstick for measuring performance and identifying areas for improvement.

To effectively set quality objectives, it is essential to follow the SMART framework – Specific, Measurable, Achievable, Relevant, and Time-bound. Specific objectives ensure clarity and focus, while measurable objectives enable quantifiable evaluation. Achievable objectives set realistic targets that can be accomplished, while relevant objectives align with the organization's overall goals. Finally, time-bound objectives establish deadlines, creating a sense of urgency and accountability.

Once quality objectives are established, the next step is to develop appropriate metrics to measure progress. Metrics provide tangible data that indicate whether the organization is on track towards achieving its quality objectives. They enable industrial engineers to analyze trends, identify bottlenecks, and make data-driven decisions for continuous improvement.

When selecting metrics, it is vital to consider both leading and lagging indicators. Leading indicators offer early warning signs of potential quality issues, allowing proactive measures to be taken. Lagging indicators, on the other hand, reflect past performance and provide insights into the effectiveness of improvement efforts. By utilizing a combination of leading and lagging indicators, industrial engineers can gain a comprehensive view of the quality landscape and take appropriate actions.

Furthermore, the choice of metrics should be tailored to the organization's specific needs and objectives. Common quality metrics include defect rates, customer satisfaction scores, on-time delivery performance, and process cycle time. These metrics should be easy to collect, analyze, and interpret, ensuring their usability for decision-making.

In conclusion, setting quality objectives and metrics is a critical aspect of mastering quality control in industrial engineering. By defining clear objectives and selecting appropriate metrics, industrial engineers can drive continuous improvement, enhance customer satisfaction, and achieve organizational excellence. This subchapter aims to equip every industrial engineer with the knowledge and tools necessary to establish effective quality objectives and metrics for success in their field.

Developing Standard Operating Procedures (SOPs)

In the world of industrial engineering, it is crucial to have well-defined and standardized processes in place to ensure consistency, efficiency, and quality. This is where Standard Operating Procedures (SOPs) come into play. SOPs serve as a set of instructions or guidelines that outline how specific tasks or activities should be performed within an organization. They act as a roadmap for employees, enabling them to carry out their duties in a uniform and effective manner.

The subchapter "Developing Standard Operating Procedures (SOPs)" in the book "Mastering Quality Control: A Guide for Industrial Engineers" is designed to provide valuable insights and guidance to individuals across various industries, regardless of their level of expertise. Whether you are an experienced industrial engineer or just starting your career, understanding the importance of SOPs and learning how to develop them can significantly enhance your operations.

The subchapter begins by explaining the fundamental concepts and principles behind SOPs. It emphasizes the significance of standardization in streamlining processes and reducing errors. Readers will learn how SOPs act as a bridge between management expectations and employee execution by providing clear instructions, minimizing deviations, and ensuring compliance with industry regulations.

Moving forward, the subchapter delves into the step-by-step process of developing SOPs. It outlines the key elements that should be included in an effective SOP, such as a clear objective, detailed procedures, safety precautions, troubleshooting guidelines, and relevant references. Additionally, it provides practical tips for writing SOPs that are concise, easy to understand, and adaptable to changing circumstances.

Furthermore, the subchapter highlights the importance of involving employees in the SOP development process. It emphasizes the benefits of collaboration and obtaining feedback from frontline workers who possess valuable insights into the day-to-day operations. By involving employees, organizations can foster a sense of ownership and commitment to the SOPs, ultimately leading to better compliance and performance.

To ensure the successful implementation of SOPs, the subchapter also covers the importance of training and communication. It discusses the significance of providing comprehensive training programs to employees, enabling them to fully understand and adopt the SOPs. Additionally, it emphasizes the need for effective communication channels to disseminate SOP updates, address concerns, and facilitate continuous improvement.

In conclusion, the subchapter "Developing Standard Operating Procedures (SOPs)" in the book "Mastering Quality Control: A Guide for Industrial Engineers" serves as a comprehensive guide for individuals in the field of industrial engineering. By understanding the principles and process of developing SOPs, readers can enhance their organization's operational efficiency, ensure consistent quality, and drive continuous improvement. This subchapter caters to a wide audience, including industrial engineers, managers, and employees across various industries, who are looking to optimize their processes and achieve excellence in their operations.

Establishing Quality Control Plans

In the field of industrial engineering, quality control plays a crucial role in ensuring that products and processes meet the highest standards of excellence. A well-established quality control plan not only helps identify and rectify any potential issues but also promotes efficiency and customer satisfaction. This subchapter aims to provide a comprehensive guide on how to establish effective quality control plans in an industrial setting.

1. Understanding Quality Control: Before diving into the specifics, it is essential to understand the concept of quality control and its significance. Quality control involves systematic activities that are implemented to ensure that products or services meet predetermined quality standards. It encompasses various techniques and methodologies to identify defects, reduce variation, and improve overall quality.

2. Defining Quality Control Objectives: The first step in establishing a quality control plan is to determine the objectives. These objectives should align with the organization's overall goals and customer expectations. Clear and measurable objectives provide a roadmap for implementing quality control measures effectively.

3. Identifying Key Quality Parameters: In any industrial process, certain parameters are critical for maintaining quality. These parameters can include dimensions, materials, performance criteria, and adherence to industry standards. Identifying and documenting these parameters is essential for establishing a robust quality control plan.

4. Developing Quality Control Procedures: Once the key quality parameters are identified, it is necessary to develop appropriate procedures for monitoring and controlling them. This may involve creating checklists, implementing statistical process control techniques, or conducting regular inspections. The procedures should be well-documented and accessible to all relevant stakeholders.

5. Training and Empowering Employees: Quality control is not solely the responsibility of a dedicated team; it involves the participation of all employees. Providing comprehensive training on quality control principles and techniques ensures that everyone understands their role in maintaining quality standards. Empowering employees to contribute to the improvement of processes and products can significantly enhance the effectiveness of a quality control plan.

6. Continuous Improvement: A quality control plan should never be considered a static document. Regular evaluations and feedback from customers and employees should be incorporated to identify areas for improvement. Implementing a culture of continuous improvement ensures that the quality control plan remains effective and relevant in a dynamic industrial environment.

By establishing a well-designed quality control plan, industrial engineers can effectively manage and enhance the quality of products and processes. This subchapter provides a comprehensive guide to help industrial engineering professionals develop and implement quality control plans that meet the highest industry standards. Whether you are new to the field or seeking to refine your existing practices, mastering quality control is an essential skill for all industrial engineers.

Documenting and Communicating Quality Procedures

In the world of industrial engineering, quality control plays a vital role in ensuring the success and efficiency of any manufacturing process. It is crucial for every individual involved in this field to understand the importance of documenting and communicating quality procedures effectively. This subchapter aims to shed light on this critical aspect of mastering quality control.

Documentation is the backbone of any quality control system. It provides a comprehensive record of procedures, guidelines, and standards that need to be followed to maintain the desired level of quality. By documenting quality procedures, industrial engineers can ensure consistency, traceability, and accountability throughout the manufacturing process.

One of the primary benefits of documenting quality procedures is the ability to establish a baseline for performance. By clearly defining the procedures, engineers can measure and evaluate the effectiveness of their quality control efforts. This documentation serves as a reference point for future improvements and helps identify areas that require attention or modification.

Furthermore, documentation plays a crucial role in ensuring compliance with industry regulations and standards. Industrial engineers must be well-versed in the relevant guidelines and regulations that pertain to their specific field. By documenting these procedures, they can ensure that all activities are in line with legal requirements, thus avoiding potential legal and financial repercussions.

While documentation is essential, it is equally important to communicate these procedures effectively. The success of any quality control system relies heavily on effective communication between all stakeholders involved. Engineers must strive to convey the documented procedures clearly and concisely, ensuring that they are easily understood and implemented by everyone.

Moreover, effective communication ensures that all team members are aware of their responsibilities and understand the impact of their actions on the quality of the final product. By fostering a culture of open communication, industrial engineers can create an environment where feedback, suggestions, and concerns can be freely shared, leading to continuous improvement in quality control processes.

In conclusion, documenting and communicating quality procedures is a fundamental aspect of mastering quality control in the field of industrial engineering. It provides a foundation for measuring performance, ensuring compliance, and fostering effective communication among all stakeholders. By prioritizing this subchapter, every industrial engineer can enhance their knowledge and skills in maintaining and improving the quality of manufacturing processes.

Implementing Quality Control Training Programs

Quality control is an essential practice in the field of industrial engineering. It ensures that products and processes meet or exceed the desired standards. However, to achieve effective quality control, it is crucial to have a well-trained workforce. This subchapter will explore the importance of implementing quality control training programs and provide guidance on how to develop and execute these programs within an industrial engineering setting.

Why Quality Control Training Programs Matter

Quality control training programs play a vital role in enhancing the overall quality management system of an organization. By equipping employees with the necessary knowledge and skills, these programs enable them to identify defects, implement corrective actions, and maintain consistent quality standards. Training programs also help in cultivating a culture of continuous improvement, ensuring that employees are constantly looking for ways to enhance quality control processes.

Developing Quality Control Training Programs

To design an effective quality control training program, it is essential to first assess the specific needs and requirements of the organization and its employees. This can be done by conducting a thorough analysis of the current quality control practices, identifying areas for improvement, and determining the skill gaps that need to be addressed. Based on this assessment, a comprehensive training curriculum can be developed, covering topics such as statistical process control, root cause analysis, quality assurance techniques, and quality management systems.

Executing Quality Control Training Programs

The successful execution of quality control training programs relies on various factors, including effective communication, engagement, and evaluation. Communication should be clear and concise, ensuring that employees understand the purpose and benefits of the training. Engagement can be achieved through interactive training methods, such as workshops, case studies, and simulations. Regular evaluations should be conducted to assess the effectiveness of the training program and identify areas that require further improvement.

Benefits of Quality Control Training Programs

Implementing quality control training programs brings several benefits to both organizations and employees. For organizations, these programs lead to improved product quality, reduced defects and waste, increased customer satisfaction, and enhanced competitiveness. Employees benefit from increased job satisfaction, better career prospects, and the ability to contribute to the organization's success.

In conclusion, implementing quality control training programs is essential for industrial engineering professionals. These programs empower employees with the knowledge and skills required to maintain and improve quality standards. By developing and executing effective training programs, organizations can ensure that their workforce is equipped to deliver products and processes that meet or exceed customer expectations.

Chapter 4: Quality Control in Manufacturing Processes

Defining Key Performance Indicators (KPIs) for Manufacturing

In the realm of industrial engineering, the pursuit of quality control is paramount. To effectively monitor and improve the performance of manufacturing processes, it is essential to define and track Key Performance Indicators (KPIs). These indicators provide valuable insights into the efficiency, effectiveness, and overall success of a manufacturing operation.

KPIs are quantifiable metrics that measure specific aspects of performance and help organizations set and achieve their objectives. By establishing KPIs, industrial engineers can gain a comprehensive understanding of the manufacturing process and identify areas for improvement. In this subchapter, we will explore the significance of defining KPIs for manufacturing and its relevance to the field of industrial engineering.

One of the primary benefits of KPIs is their ability to reflect the performance of various manufacturing processes. By carefully selecting relevant indicators, industrial engineers can assess the effectiveness of production lines, equipment, and workforce. This enables them to identify bottlenecks, streamline operations, and optimize resource allocation. Additionally, KPIs facilitate data-driven decision-making, as they provide a clear benchmark against which performance can be measured.

Defining KPIs for manufacturing requires a systematic approach. Firstly, industrial engineers must identify the specific goals they wish to achieve. These objectives may include reducing defects, improving productivity, enhancing customer satisfaction, or minimizing costs. Once the goals are established, the next step is to determine the most suitable metrics to track progress towards these objectives. Common KPIs in manufacturing include Overall Equipment Efficiency (OEE), defect rate, cycle time, and customer returns.

Selecting the right KPIs is crucial, as they should align with the organization's overall strategy and objectives. Furthermore, KPIs should be measurable, relevant, and actionable. By regularly monitoring these indicators, industrial engineers can identify trends, patterns, and areas of concern. This allows for proactive decision-making and the implementation of corrective measures before issues escalate.

Overall, defining KPIs for manufacturing is essential for industrial engineers to effectively monitor and improve the performance of manufacturing processes. By selecting relevant metrics and regularly tracking them, organizations can make data-driven decisions, optimize resource allocation, and achieve their quality control objectives. In the ever-evolving field of industrial engineering, mastering the art of defining and utilizing KPIs is crucial for success.

Process Mapping and Analysis

Introduction:

In the realm of industrial engineering, one of the key aspects of ensuring quality control is through process mapping and analysis. This subchapter delves into the significance of process mapping and analysis in optimizing operations and achieving desired outcomes. Whether you're an industrial engineer, a business owner, or simply interested in improving processes, understanding this fundamental concept is paramount.

Understanding Process Mapping:

Process mapping involves visually representing a series of steps or activities undertaken to complete a specific task or achieve a desired outcome. By mapping out processes, industrial engineers gain a comprehensive understanding of how inputs are transformed into outputs, identifying areas for improvement and optimization.

Benefits of Process Mapping and Analysis:

1. Improved Efficiency: Process mapping enables industrial engineers to identify bottlenecks, redundancies, and unnecessary steps in a workflow. By eliminating or streamlining these inefficiencies, organizations can significantly improve productivity and reduce costs.

2. Enhanced Quality: Mapping and analyzing processes allows for the identification of potential quality issues, enabling engineers to implement preventive measures. By addressing quality concerns at the

source, organizations can minimize defects and enhance overall product or service quality.

3. Effective Resource Allocation: Process mapping helps to identify resource utilization patterns. This enables industrial engineers to allocate resources optimally, ensuring that each step in the process receives the necessary inputs without wastage.

4. Streamlined Communication: Visual representations of processes facilitate effective communication among team members, departments, and stakeholders. Process maps provide a shared understanding of the workflow, enabling seamless coordination and collaboration.

Process Analysis Techniques:

1. Value Stream Mapping (VSM): VSM focuses on identifying value-added and non-value-added activities in a process. By eliminating non-value-added steps, organizations can reduce lead times, improve efficiency, and enhance customer satisfaction.

2. Six Sigma: This approach aims to reduce process variation and defects. By using statistical tools and methodologies, industrial engineers can measure, analyze, and improve processes systematically.

3. Root Cause Analysis (RCA): RCA enables engineers to identify the underlying causes of process failures or quality issues. By addressing these root causes, organizations can prevent recurrence and improve overall process performance.

Conclusion:

Process mapping and analysis are vital tools for industrial engineers and organizations seeking to optimize processes and achieve quality control. By mapping out workflows, identifying inefficiencies, and utilizing various analysis techniques, organizations can enhance efficiency, quality, resource allocation, and communication. Regardless of your role or industry, understanding and implementing process mapping and analysis can lead to significant improvements and ultimately contribute to the success of your endeavors.

Identifying and Eliminating Waste in Manufacturing

In the realm of Industrial Engineering, one of the key objectives is to optimize manufacturing processes to ensure maximum efficiency and productivity. Waste management plays a pivotal role in achieving this goal. In this subchapter, we will explore the various types of waste that can occur in manufacturing and provide strategies for identifying and eliminating them.

Waste, in the context of manufacturing, refers to any activity or resource that does not add value to the final product. These wastes can manifest in several forms, commonly known as the 7 Wastes or 7 Mudas: overproduction, waiting, transportation, inappropriate processing, excess inventory, unnecessary motion, and defects. Recognizing these wastes is crucial to streamlining operations and reducing costs.

To identify waste in manufacturing, it is essential to conduct thorough observations and analysis of the production process. This involves closely examining each step, from the arrival of raw materials to the final product delivery. Engaging the workforce, including operators and supervisors, in this process can provide valuable insights as they are intimately familiar with the daily operations and may have ideas for improvement.

Once waste has been identified, it is time to eliminate or minimize it. Lean manufacturing techniques, such as the 5S methodology and value stream mapping, can be employed to achieve this objective. The 5S methodology focuses on organizing the workplace, reducing clutter, and creating a clean and efficient work environment. Value stream mapping allows for the visualization and analysis of the entire production process, enabling the identification of bottlenecks and areas of improvement.

In addition to Lean principles, other strategies can be implemented to eliminate waste. Just-in-Time (JIT) manufacturing, for example, aims to reduce inventory and minimize waiting time by delivering materials and components precisely when they are needed. Kaizen, a Japanese term for continuous improvement, encourages small, incremental changes in processes to eliminate waste over time. Quality control tools, such as statistical process control and Six Sigma, can be utilized to identify and eliminate defects, reducing waste and improving overall product quality.

By identifying and eliminating waste in manufacturing, Industrial Engineers can significantly enhance productivity, reduce costs, and improve the quality of products. This not only benefits the organization but also contributes to sustainable and eco-friendly practices by reducing resource consumption and waste generation. Embracing waste management as an integral part of the manufacturing process is essential for any industrial engineer looking to master quality control and drive continuous improvement.

Standardizing Work Instructions

In the field of industrial engineering, one of the key factors in ensuring efficiency, productivity, and quality control is standardizing work instructions. Work instructions provide a detailed step-by-step guide for employees to follow when performing their tasks, ensuring consistency and uniformity in the work processes. This subchapter will delve into the importance of standardizing work instructions and how it can benefit industries across the board.

Standardization of work instructions is crucial as it eliminates ambiguity and confusion, allowing employees to clearly understand their tasks and expectations. When work instructions are not standardized, different individuals may interpret instructions differently, leading to variations in the work performed. This can result in inconsistencies in quality, increased error rates, and reduced productivity. By standardizing work instructions, companies can minimize these risks and create a systematic approach to tasks, resulting in improved overall performance.

Moreover, standardizing work instructions enables companies to achieve greater efficiency. When employees follow a consistent set of instructions, they can optimize their workflow and reduce unnecessary steps or redundant activities. This streamlines the processes, eliminates waste, and maximizes output. Consequently, industries adopting standardized work instructions often experience improved productivity and reduced costs.

Standardization also plays a critical role in quality control. By having consistent work instructions, companies can establish a baseline for quality and monitor deviations from it. This allows them to identify and rectify issues promptly, preventing defects or errors from reaching the customers. With standardized work instructions, companies can establish quality control measures and monitor performance effectively, ensuring that products or services consistently meet or exceed customer expectations.

Furthermore, standardizing work instructions facilitates employee training and onboarding. New employees can easily learn their tasks by following standardized instructions, reducing the learning curve and enabling them to contribute to the organization's goals more quickly. Additionally, standardized work instructions can serve as a reference for employees, enabling them to refresh their knowledge or troubleshoot issues independently.

In conclusion, standardizing work instructions is a fundamental aspect of industrial engineering that benefits industries across various niches. By providing clear, consistent, and well-defined instructions, companies can enhance productivity, improve quality control, reduce costs, and streamline their operations. It is essential for every industrial engineer and industry professional to recognize the importance of standardizing work instructions and implement this practice to achieve optimal performance and success.

Implementing Continuous Improvement Initiatives

Continuous improvement is an essential aspect of industrial engineering, as it allows organizations to enhance their processes, products, and services over time. By regularly evaluating and refining existing practices, companies can drive efficiencies, reduce waste, and ultimately increase customer satisfaction. This subchapter aims to guide industrial engineers in implementing effective continuous improvement initiatives within their organizations.

1. Understanding the Importance of Continuous Improvement: Continuous improvement is not just a buzzword; it is a strategic approach that fosters a culture of innovation and drives long-term success. By emphasizing the need for ongoing enhancements, industrial engineers can ensure their organizations remain competitive in today's rapidly evolving business landscape.

2. Setting Clear Objectives and Key Performance Indicators (KPIs): To implement effective continuous improvement initiatives, it is vital to define clear objectives and KPIs. These metrics will act as benchmarks to assess progress and identify areas for improvement. By aligning goals with the organization's overall strategy, industrial engineers can ensure that improvement efforts are directed towards meaningful outcomes.

3. Engaging and Empowering Employees: Successful continuous improvement initiatives require the active participation and engagement of all employees. Industrial engineers should foster a culture of collaboration and empower team members to contribute their ideas and insights. By soliciting input from those

directly involved in the processes, engineers can identify improvement opportunities that might otherwise go unnoticed.

4. Implementing Lean Principles: Industrial engineers should leverage lean principles such as value stream mapping, 5S, and Kaizen to drive continuous improvement. By visualizing and analyzing the entire value stream, engineers can identify bottlenecks, eliminate waste, and streamline processes. Regular Kaizen events can also provide a structured approach to tackle specific improvement projects.

5. Using Data and Analytics for Decision-making: Data-driven decision-making is crucial to successful continuous improvement. Industrial engineers must collect and analyze relevant data to identify patterns, trends, and areas for improvement. By leveraging technology and advanced analytics tools, engineers can identify improvement opportunities, monitor progress, and make informed decisions based on factual evidence.

6. Implementing Change Management Strategies: Introducing and sustaining continuous improvement initiatives can be challenging. Industrial engineers should develop effective change management strategies to ensure buy-in and support from all stakeholders. Communicating the benefits, providing adequate training, and addressing concerns will help overcome resistance and foster a positive attitude towards change.

In conclusion, implementing continuous improvement initiatives is a fundamental aspect of industrial engineering. By setting clear objectives, engaging employees, implementing lean principles, utilizing data, and employing effective change management strategies, industrial engineers can drive ongoing enhancements within their organizations. Embracing a culture of continuous improvement will enable companies to remain competitive, improve customer satisfaction, and achieve long-term success in today's dynamic business environment.

Chapter 5: Quality Control in Supply Chain Management

Ensuring Supplier Quality

In the world of industrial engineering, maintaining a high level of quality is paramount to the success of any project or production process. One of the key aspects of achieving this goal is ensuring supplier quality. This subchapter will delve into the various strategies and techniques that can be employed to guarantee that the materials and components received from suppliers meet the required standards.

The first step in ensuring supplier quality is to establish clear and concise specifications for the desired materials or components. This involves collaborating with suppliers to identify the necessary characteristics, tolerances, and performance requirements. By clearly defining these specifications, the chances of receiving subpar or inadequate supplies can be greatly minimized.

Once the specifications are in place, it is crucial to implement a robust supplier evaluation process. This involves conducting thorough assessments of potential suppliers before entering into any contractual agreements. Evaluations can include a review of the supplier's quality management system, their track record of delivering on time, their financial stability, and their compliance with industry regulations. By selecting suppliers who meet these criteria, the risk of receiving low-quality supplies is significantly reduced.

Another effective strategy for ensuring supplier quality is to establish a strong and open line of communication. Regular and transparent communication with suppliers can help to build a strong relationship based on trust and cooperation. This can involve discussing any concerns or issues that may arise, as well as providing feedback on the quality of the supplies received. By fostering a collaborative and communicative environment, suppliers will be more inclined to address any quality-related problems promptly.

In addition to communication, regular audits and inspections of suppliers' facilities can provide valuable insights into their manufacturing processes and quality control measures. These audits can help to identify any potential weaknesses or areas for improvement, allowing for early intervention and proactive measures to be taken. By ensuring that suppliers adhere to stringent quality standards, the risk of receiving defective or non-compliant supplies can be minimized.

Lastly, it is essential to establish a feedback loop for continuous improvement. By monitoring and analyzing the performance of suppliers over time, patterns and trends can be identified. This data can then be used to develop strategies for enhancing supplier quality, such as providing training or implementing corrective actions.

In conclusion, ensuring supplier quality is a vital aspect of industrial engineering. By establishing clear specifications, conducting thorough evaluations, fostering open communication, conducting audits, and implementing continuous improvement measures, the risk of receiving subpar supplies can be mitigated. By diligently following these strategies, industrial engineers can contribute to the overall success and quality of their projects and production processes.

Vendor Evaluation and Performance Monitoring

In today's fast-paced and competitive business world, industrial engineers play a crucial role in ensuring the success and efficiency of manufacturing processes. One essential aspect of their work is vendor evaluation and performance monitoring. This subchapter will delve into the significance of vendor evaluation, its benefits, and the strategies for effective performance monitoring.

Vendor evaluation is the process of assessing the capabilities, reliability, and performance of suppliers or vendors. It is vital for industrial engineers to thoroughly evaluate potential vendors before engaging in any business transactions. By conducting a comprehensive evaluation, engineers can select vendors that align with their company's goals, requirements, and quality standards.

The benefits of vendor evaluation are manifold. Firstly, it helps industrial engineers identify vendors who can consistently deliver high-quality products or services. This ensures that the company receives reliable and defect-free inputs, which is crucial for maintaining quality control throughout the production process. Secondly, evaluating vendors enables engineers to identify potential risks and take preventive measures to mitigate them. This proactive approach helps in avoiding production delays, product defects, or any other issues that may arise due to unreliable vendors.

To perform effective vendor evaluation, industrial engineers should consider various factors such as a vendor's financial stability, production capacity, quality control measures, and track record. Additionally, engineers should also assess vendors' responsiveness, communication skills, and ability to meet deadlines. By considering these factors, engineers can make informed decisions and select vendors who can meet their specific requirements.

Once vendors are selected, the process of performance monitoring becomes crucial. Industrial engineers need to establish a robust monitoring system to ensure that vendors consistently meet the predetermined quality standards. This involves setting key performance indicators (KPIs) and regularly assessing and reviewing vendor performance against these metrics. By closely monitoring vendors, engineers can quickly identify any deviations or non-compliance and take corrective actions promptly.

In conclusion, vendor evaluation and performance monitoring are critical components of industrial engineering. By thoroughly evaluating vendors and establishing a robust monitoring system, engineers can ensure that their company receives high-quality inputs and maintains efficient production processes. This subchapter aims to provide essential insights and strategies for mastering vendor evaluation and performance monitoring in the field of industrial engineering.

Implementing Effective Supplier Audits

In the realm of industrial engineering, ensuring the quality and reliability of the products and materials sourced from suppliers is paramount. To achieve this, implementing effective supplier audits is essential. Supplier audits not only help in assessing the capability and compliance of suppliers but also play a crucial role in maintaining consistent quality control throughout the supply chain.

The purpose of conducting supplier audits is to evaluate the supplier's ability to meet the specified quality requirements, adherence to industry standards, and compliance with regulatory guidelines. By conducting regular audits, industrial engineers can identify potential risks, mitigate them, and proactively work towards improving the quality of the supplied materials.

The first step in implementing effective supplier audits is to establish clear criteria and standards for evaluation. These criteria should be aligned with the quality goals of the organization and should cover aspects such as production processes, quality management systems, documentation, and product specifications. Once the criteria are defined, a checklist can be created to facilitate the audit process.

The next step involves selecting the appropriate audit method. There are various audit methods available, such as on-site audits, remote audits, and third-party audits. Each method has its advantages and limitations, and the choice depends on factors like the scale of the supplier's operations, geographical location, and available resources. On-site audits are typically more comprehensive and allow for direct observations, while remote audits can be cost-effective and efficient for suppliers located in distant regions.

During the audit, it is essential to engage in effective communication with the supplier. Clear and open communication helps in building a collaborative relationship and fosters a better understanding of expectations and requirements. The audit team should interact with the supplier's management, quality assurance personnel, and production staff to gain insights into the supplier's operations, quality practices, and quality control measures.

Once the audit is completed, it is crucial to document the findings comprehensively. The audit report should include observations, non-conformities, areas of improvement, and recommendations for corrective actions. This report serves as a valuable reference for the supplier and the organization to track progress and monitor improvements over time.

Implementing effective supplier audits not only ensures the quality of the supplied products but also helps in building trust and long-term partnerships with suppliers. By proactively addressing quality issues, industrial engineers can minimize risks, reduce costs, and enhance customer satisfaction.

Managing Product Quality throughout the Supply Chain

In today's globalized world, managing product quality throughout the supply chain has become an essential aspect of industrial engineering. It is no longer sufficient to focus solely on quality control within the four walls of a manufacturing facility; instead, a holistic approach must be adopted to ensure consistent quality at every stage of the supply chain. This subchapter explores the various strategies and techniques that industrial engineers can employ to effectively manage product quality throughout the entire supply chain.

One of the key elements of managing product quality is establishing a comprehensive quality management system (QMS) that encompasses all stages of the supply chain. This involves developing and implementing quality standards, procedures, and guidelines that are adhered to by all suppliers, manufacturers, and distributors. By having a well-defined QMS in place, industrial engineers can ensure that quality requirements are clearly communicated, understood, and followed by all stakeholders.

Another crucial aspect of managing product quality throughout the supply chain is conducting regular audits and inspections. Industrial engineers should regularly assess the performance of suppliers, manufacturers, and distributors to identify any potential quality issues. By conducting thorough audits and inspections, they can identify non-conformances, deviations, and areas for improvement, allowing for timely corrective actions to be taken.

In addition to audits and inspections, effective communication and collaboration among all stakeholders are essential for managing product quality. Industrial engineers should establish strong relationships with suppliers, manufacturers, and distributors, fostering an environment of trust and open communication. Regular meetings, performance reviews, and feedback sessions can help ensure that all parties are aligned on quality expectations and can address any issues promptly.

Furthermore, leveraging technology and data analytics can significantly enhance the management of product quality throughout the supply chain. Industrial engineers can utilize advanced quality control tools and software to track and analyze data related to product performance, supplier performance, and customer feedback. This data-driven approach enables them to identify trends, patterns, and potential risks, allowing for proactive quality management.

In conclusion, managing product quality throughout the supply chain is of utmost importance in the field of industrial engineering. By establishing a comprehensive QMS, conducting regular audits and inspections, fostering strong relationships, and leveraging technology, industrial engineers can ensure consistent and high-quality products throughout the entire supply chain. This subchapter has provided an overview of the strategies and techniques that can be employed to achieve this goal, empowering industrial engineers to master quality control in today's complex and interconnected world.

Reducing Lead Time and Enhancing Delivery Performance

In today's fast-paced and competitive business environment, reducing lead time and enhancing delivery performance are crucial factors for success in the field of industrial engineering. Whether you are a professional in the industry or a student aspiring to join this dynamic field, mastering these skills is essential to stay ahead of the curve and deliver exceptional results.

Lead time refers to the time taken from the initiation of a process until its completion. It includes the time required for processing, manufacturing, and delivering a product or service to the customer. By reducing lead time, organizations can not only improve customer satisfaction but also gain a competitive advantage by responding quickly to market demands.

One of the key strategies to reduce lead time is through effective process optimization. Industrial engineers play a vital role in analyzing and streamlining various processes across different stages of production. By eliminating unnecessary steps, improving workflow, and adopting lean manufacturing principles, lead time can be significantly reduced.

Enhancing delivery performance is equally important in industrial engineering. It involves ensuring that products are delivered to customers on time and in optimal condition. This requires efficient coordination between different departments, such as production, logistics, and quality control. Industrial engineers can leverage their expertise in supply chain management and logistics to optimize delivery routes, minimize transportation costs, and ensure timely delivery.

Moreover, embracing technology and automation can greatly enhance delivery performance. Industrial engineers can implement advanced software solutions, such as enterprise resource planning (ERP) systems, to streamline communication, track inventory, and monitor production progress. This not only improves delivery performance but also enables real-time data analysis for continuous improvement.

It is essential for industrial engineers to constantly evaluate and analyze delivery performance metrics. By measuring key performance indicators (KPIs) such as on-time delivery, delivery accuracy, and customer satisfaction, engineers can identify areas for improvement and implement corrective actions.

In conclusion, reducing lead time and enhancing delivery performance are critical aspects of industrial engineering. By optimizing processes, leveraging technology, and continuously evaluating performance metrics, industrial engineers can drive efficiency, improve customer satisfaction, and achieve long-term success in the field. Whether you are a professional or a student, mastering these skills is vital for staying competitive in the ever-evolving industrial engineering industry.

Chapter 6: Quality Control in Service Industries

Understanding the Unique Challenges of Service Quality Control

In the field of industrial engineering, quality control is a critical aspect that ensures products meet the desired standards. However, when it comes to service quality control, a unique set of challenges arises. This subchapter aims to shed light on these challenges and provide insights into how industrial engineers can effectively navigate them.

Unlike tangible products, services are intangible and highly variable, making it difficult to establish consistent quality standards. Service quality control requires a different approach, as it involves managing the customer experience and meeting their expectations. Industrial engineers must understand the intricacies of service delivery and devise strategies to ensure consistent quality.

One of the primary challenges faced in service quality control is the human factor. Services are delivered by people, and their performance can significantly impact the overall quality. Industrial engineers must focus on hiring and training the right personnel, equipping them with the necessary skills and knowledge to deliver high-quality services consistently. Implementing performance management systems can help monitor and assess the performance of service employees, identifying areas for improvement and providing necessary training interventions.

Another unique challenge is the intangibility of services. Unlike physical products, services cannot be seen or touched, making it challenging to measure their quality objectively. Industrial engineers must develop innovative methods to gauge service quality, such as customer surveys, feedback systems, and mystery shopping. These tools can provide valuable insights into customer satisfaction levels and identify areas where service improvements are needed.

Service variability is yet another challenge in quality control. Services are highly dependent on the specific context in which they are delivered, leading to variations in quality. Industrial engineers must focus on standardizing processes and reducing variability by implementing robust quality control measures. This can involve designing and implementing service delivery protocols, ensuring consistency across different service providers and locations.

Additionally, managing customer expectations is crucial in service quality control. Customers have varying expectations, and meeting or exceeding these expectations is crucial for ensuring customer satisfaction. Industrial engineers must work closely with marketing teams to understand customer expectations and develop strategies to consistently meet or exceed them. Effective communication and setting clear service standards are essential in managing customer expectations and maintaining service quality.

In conclusion, service quality control poses unique challenges for industrial engineers in the field of industrial engineering. By understanding these challenges and implementing appropriate strategies, industrial engineers can ensure consistent service quality and customer satisfaction. This subchapter serves as a guide to navigating these challenges, providing insights and practical tips for mastering service quality control in the industrial engineering field.

Developing Service Quality Standards

In today's competitive business landscape, service quality plays a crucial role in the success of any organization. In the field of industrial engineering, ensuring high service quality is vital to meet customer expectations and maintain a competitive edge. This subchapter aims to provide a comprehensive guide on developing service quality standards, equipping industrial engineers with the necessary tools to optimize their processes and deliver exceptional service to their clients.

The first step in developing service quality standards is to understand the specific needs and expectations of the target audience. This includes conducting thorough market research, customer surveys, and analyzing feedback to identify key areas for improvement. By gaining a deep understanding of customer requirements, industrial engineers can tailor their service quality standards to meet and exceed expectations.

Once the customer needs are identified, the next step is to define measurable objectives and performance indicators. These should align with the organization's overall goals and reflect the desired outcomes of the service. Industrial engineers can utilize various quality management tools, such as the SERVQUAL model or the Kano model, to establish benchmarks and track performance against these standards.

To ensure consistent service quality, it is essential to establish clear processes and procedures. This involves mapping out the entire service delivery process, identifying potential bottlenecks or areas prone to errors, and implementing effective controls to mitigate risks.

Standard operating procedures (SOPs) can be developed to guide employees in delivering the service with consistency and efficiency.

Furthermore, industrial engineers should focus on training and development programs to equip employees with the necessary skills and knowledge to deliver high-quality service. Regular performance evaluations and feedback sessions can help identify areas of improvement and provide opportunities for continuous learning and development.

In the rapidly evolving landscape of industrial engineering, incorporating technology into service quality standards is crucial. Industrial engineers should leverage automation, data analytics, and innovative technologies to streamline processes, identify trends, and proactively address potential issues. This can lead to improved efficiency, reduced errors, and enhanced customer satisfaction.

To conclude, developing service quality standards is an integral part of industrial engineering. By understanding customer requirements, setting measurable objectives, establishing clear processes, investing in employee training, and utilizing technology, industrial engineers can consistently deliver exceptional service and stay ahead in a competitive market.

Conducting Service Process Audits

In the realm of industrial engineering, ensuring the quality and efficiency of service processes is crucial for organizations to thrive and deliver exceptional customer experiences. This subchapter explores the concept of conducting service process audits and provides valuable insights for industrial engineers seeking to master quality control.

Service process audits involve a systematic examination of service processes to identify areas of improvement, eliminate inefficiencies, and enhance overall performance. These audits play a vital role in maintaining and improving the quality of services delivered to customers. By analyzing and evaluating various aspects of service processes, industrial engineers can identify bottlenecks, non-value-added activities, and potential sources of errors or delays.

When conducting a service process audit, industrial engineers should begin by defining the objectives and scope of the audit. This includes identifying the specific service processes to be audited, determining the desired outcomes, and establishing key performance indicators (KPIs) to measure success. It is essential to involve relevant stakeholders, including service managers, frontline employees, and even customers, to gain a comprehensive understanding of the service processes.

During the audit, industrial engineers employ various techniques to assess the effectiveness and efficiency of service processes. These may include process mapping, data analysis, observation, interviews, and customer feedback analysis. By using these tools, engineers can identify process variations, deviations from standard operating procedures, employee skill gaps, and areas where automation or technology integration can streamline operations.

The audit findings serve as a foundation for developing improvement strategies and implementing corrective actions. Industrial engineers collaborate with service managers and employees to devise and prioritize solutions that align with organizational goals and customer expectations. Continuous monitoring and follow-up audits are essential to ensure the effectiveness of implemented improvements and to address any emerging issues.

Conducting service process audits is not a one-time activity but a continuous effort to achieve and maintain service excellence. By embracing a culture of regular auditing, industrial engineers can drive continuous improvement, enhance customer satisfaction, and ultimately contribute to the overall success of the organization.

In conclusion, service process audits are an integral part of quality control for industrial engineers in the field of industrial engineering. By examining service processes, identifying areas for improvement, and implementing corrective actions, engineers can optimize efficiency, eliminate waste, and deliver exceptional service experiences to customers. Through continuous monitoring and improvement, organizations can stay ahead in a competitive market and achieve sustainable success in the realm of industrial engineering.

Implementing Quality Control in Service Delivery

Quality control is an essential aspect of any industry, and it plays a significant role in ensuring customer satisfaction. In the field of industrial engineering, the concept of quality control is equally important, especially when it comes to service delivery. This subchapter aims to provide a comprehensive guide on implementing quality control in service delivery, specifically tailored for industrial engineers.

Service delivery encompasses a wide range of industries, including healthcare, transportation, hospitality, and customer service. Regardless of the industry, the primary objective is to meet or exceed customer expectations consistently. Implementing quality control measures ensures that services are delivered efficiently, effectively, and to the highest standards.

The first step in implementing quality control in service delivery is understanding customer requirements. Industrial engineers need to gather customer feedback, conduct surveys, and analyze market trends to identify the specific needs and expectations of their target audience. This information will serve as the foundation for designing processes and procedures that align with customer demands.

Once customer requirements are clearly defined, the next step is to establish performance metrics and standards. Industrial engineers should identify key performance indicators (KPIs) that measure the quality of service delivery. These metrics may include response time, error rates, customer satisfaction scores, and other relevant parameters. Setting benchmarks for these metrics will help evaluate the effectiveness of quality control initiatives.

To ensure consistent service quality, industrial engineers should develop robust processes and standard operating procedures (SOPs). These SOPs outline the step-by-step guidelines for delivering services and should incorporate quality control measures at every stage. Regular monitoring and auditing of these processes will help identify any deviations and take corrective actions promptly.

Furthermore, implementing quality control in service delivery requires a strong focus on employee training and development. Industrial engineers should provide comprehensive training programs that equip employees with the necessary skills and knowledge to deliver services with precision and efficiency. Regular performance evaluations and feedback sessions will help identify areas for improvement and address any skill gaps.

Continuous improvement is a fundamental aspect of quality control in service delivery. Industrial engineers should encourage a culture of innovation and learning within their organizations. This can be achieved through regular brainstorming sessions, process reviews, and the implementation of new technologies or methodologies that enhance service quality.

In conclusion, implementing quality control in service delivery is crucial for industrial engineers in various sectors. By understanding customer requirements, establishing performance metrics, developing robust processes, investing in employee training, and promoting a culture of continuous improvement, industrial engineers can ensure that their services consistently meet or exceed customer expectations. This subchapter serves as a guide to help industrial engineers master the art of quality control in service delivery, ultimately leading to enhanced customer satisfaction and business success.

Managing Customer Feedback and Complaints

Introduction

In today's highly competitive business environment, industrial engineers understand that customer satisfaction is of utmost importance for the success of any organization. Customer feedback and complaints provide valuable insights into the quality of products and services, enabling organizations to identify areas for improvement and enhance customer experiences. This subchapter aims to guide industrial engineers in effectively managing customer feedback and complaints to optimize overall quality control efforts.

Understanding the Importance of Customer Feedback

Customer feedback is a valuable resource that can help industrial engineers gain a deeper understanding of customer expectations and preferences. By actively listening to customers, engineers can identify recurring issues, patterns, and trends that may impact product quality or customer satisfaction. This feedback loop fosters an environment of continuous improvement, enabling engineers to address issues promptly and implement necessary changes.

Establishing a Feedback Mechanism

To effectively manage customer feedback, industrial engineers must establish a robust feedback mechanism. This can be achieved through various channels such as online surveys, suggestion boxes, customer support hotlines, or social media platforms. By providing multiple avenues for customers to voice their opinions, engineers can capture a wider range of feedback and ensure that it is easily accessible.

Analyzing and Categorizing Feedback

Once customer feedback is received, engineers need to analyze and categorize it to identify common themes or recurring issues. This can be achieved through data analysis techniques, including text mining and sentiment analysis. By categorizing feedback into different areas such as product quality, delivery, or customer service, engineers can identify the most critical areas for improvement and prioritize their efforts accordingly.

Taking Action and Resolving Complaints

Industrial engineers must promptly address customer complaints to demonstrate their commitment to quality and customer satisfaction. Complaints should be acknowledged and resolved in a timely manner, ensuring clear communication with the customer throughout the process. Engineers should document and analyze complaint resolutions to identify systemic issues and implement preventive measures to avoid similar complaints in the future.

Continuous Improvement through Feedback

Customer feedback and complaints should not be seen as negative aspects but rather as opportunities for improvement. Industrial engineers should encourage an organizational culture that values feedback and actively seeks it out. By incorporating customer feedback into the quality control process, engineers can continuously improve products and services, enhance customer satisfaction, and gain a competitive edge in the market.

Conclusion

Managing customer feedback and complaints is essential for industrial engineers to ensure the quality of products and services in the highly competitive industrial engineering sector. By establishing a robust feedback mechanism, analyzing and categorizing feedback, and promptly addressing complaints, engineers can enhance customer satisfaction and drive continuous improvement. Embracing customer feedback as a valuable resource will enable industrial engineers to stay ahead in the rapidly evolving business landscape and master quality control.

Chapter 7: Quality Control and Continuous Improvement Culture

Fostering a Culture of Quality in Industrial Engineering

In the field of Industrial Engineering, the pursuit of quality is of utmost importance. A culture of quality is not only essential for the success of any organization, but it also ensures the satisfaction of customers and the overall improvement of processes and products. In this subchapter, we will explore the significance of fostering a culture of quality in industrial engineering and how it can be achieved.

First and foremost, it is crucial to understand what a culture of quality entails. It goes beyond simply meeting the required standards; it involves a mindset shift that prioritizes continuous improvement, innovation, and the involvement of every individual within the organization. A culture of quality creates an environment where employees are encouraged to take ownership of their work, identify and address potential issues, and strive for excellence.

The benefits of fostering a culture of quality are numerous. Improved product quality leads to increased customer satisfaction, loyalty, and ultimately, repeat business. It also reduces the risk of recalls, defects, and waste, which can significantly impact the bottom line. Furthermore, a culture of quality enhances teamwork, communication, and employee morale, leading to higher productivity and a positive work environment.

So, how can industrial engineers foster a culture of quality? It starts with leadership commitment and support. Executives and managers must actively promote and champion quality initiatives, emphasizing its importance and integrating it into the organization's mission and values. This sets the tone and sends a clear message that quality is not just a department's responsibility but a shared goal.

Training and education are also vital components. Industrial engineers should invest in continuous learning and development opportunities for themselves and their teams. This includes staying updated on the latest quality management techniques, tools, and methodologies. By equipping themselves with the necessary knowledge and skills, they can effectively drive quality improvement initiatives and lead by example.

Another crucial aspect is the implementation of quality management systems and tools. Industrial engineers should familiarize themselves with quality frameworks such as Six Sigma, Lean, and Total Quality Management. These methodologies provide a structured approach to identify and eliminate waste, reduce variation, and enhance overall efficiency and effectiveness.

Lastly, communication and collaboration play a pivotal role in fostering a culture of quality. Industrial engineers should actively engage with cross-functional teams, involving employees from different departments in quality improvement projects. This not only encourages a shared responsibility but also promotes a sense of ownership and accountability for quality outcomes.

In conclusion, fostering a culture of quality is essential for industrial engineers in achieving organizational success and customer satisfaction. By prioritizing continuous improvement, investing in training and education, implementing quality management systems, and promoting collaboration, industrial engineers can create an environment where quality becomes ingrained in every process and everyone's mindset.

Strategies for Employee Engagement in Quality Control

In today's competitive business landscape, employee engagement plays a crucial role in ensuring the success of quality control initiatives within an organization. Industrial engineers, as key drivers of efficiency and productivity, must understand and implement effective strategies to engage employees in quality control processes. This subchapter aims to provide insights and practical tips for industrial engineers to enhance employee engagement and drive quality improvement.

1. Establish a Culture of Quality: Industrial engineers should foster a culture that emphasizes the importance of quality control. This involves setting clear quality goals, encouraging continuous improvement, and recognizing and rewarding employees for their contributions to quality.

2. Communicate the Value of Quality Control: It is essential to communicate the benefits of quality control to employees at all levels. Explain how their involvement contributes to the overall success of the organization, customer satisfaction, and long-term growth. This enables employees to understand the purpose behind quality control efforts and motivates them to actively participate.

3. Provide Training and Development: Invest in training programs to equip employees with the necessary knowledge and skills to excel in quality control. Offer workshops, seminars, and online courses that cover various quality control techniques, problem-solving methodologies, and statistical analysis tools. Continuous learning opportunities not only enhance employees' capabilities but also

demonstrate the organization's commitment to their professional growth.

4. Empower Employees: Give employees the autonomy to make decisions and take ownership of quality control processes. Encourage them to identify and address quality issues, suggest improvements, and implement innovative solutions. Empowered employees feel valued and are more likely to be engaged in quality control activities.

5. Foster Collaboration: Create cross-functional teams that bring together employees from different departments to collaborate on quality control projects. Encourage open communication, knowledge sharing, and brainstorming sessions to foster a culture of collaboration. This approach not only enhances the effectiveness of quality control efforts but also promotes a sense of shared responsibility and accountability.

6. Recognize and Reward Achievements: Celebrate employee contributions to quality control by recognizing and rewarding their achievements. Establish an incentive program that acknowledges individuals or teams who consistently demonstrate excellence in quality control. Publicly acknowledge their efforts through newsletters, emails, or company-wide meetings, and consider financial or non-financial rewards to further motivate and engage employees.

By implementing these strategies, industrial engineers can foster a culture of employee engagement in quality control. Engaged employees are more likely to embrace quality control processes, take ownership of their work, and contribute to continuous improvement efforts. Ultimately, this leads to enhanced product and service quality, increased customer satisfaction, and improved organizational performance.

Continuous Improvement Tools and Techniques

In the ever-evolving field of industrial engineering, continuous improvement is a vital component for success. It is a philosophy that emphasizes the constant search for ways to enhance processes, increase efficiency, and deliver higher quality products and services. To achieve this, various tools and techniques have been developed to assist industrial engineers in their pursuit of continuous improvement.

One such tool is the Plan-Do-Check-Act (PDCA) cycle, also known as the Deming cycle. This iterative four-step process involves planning, implementing, evaluating, and refining actions. It provides a structured approach for problem-solving and decision-making, allowing engineers to identify areas for improvement, test potential solutions, and measure the impact of changes.

Another valuable technique is Six Sigma, a data-driven methodology focused on eliminating defects and minimizing variations in processes. By employing statistical analysis and measurement tools, industrial engineers can identify root causes of problems, reduce process variability, and achieve higher levels of quality and efficiency.

Furthermore, the 5 Whys technique is an effective tool for problem-solving and root cause analysis. By repeatedly asking "why" to dig deeper into the underlying causes of a problem, industrial engineers can uncover the true source of an issue and develop targeted solutions. This technique promotes a deeper understanding of problems, leading to more effective and sustainable improvements.

Additionally, Value Stream Mapping (VSM) is a visual tool used to analyze and improve the flow of materials and information within a process or system. By mapping out the entire value stream, industrial engineers can identify areas of waste, bottlenecks, and non-value-added activities. This enables them to streamline processes, reduce lead times, and increase overall productivity.

Continuous improvement tools and techniques are not limited to these examples. Other notable tools include Statistical Process Control (SPC), Kanban systems, Total Productive Maintenance (TPM), and Lean Manufacturing principles, among many others. The choice of tool or technique depends on the specific needs and challenges faced by industrial engineers in their respective industries.

In conclusion, continuous improvement tools and techniques play a critical role in the field of industrial engineering. By adopting these approaches, engineers can identify inefficiencies, reduce waste, and enhance overall performance. The application of these tools and techniques facilitates a culture of continuous improvement, ensuring that organizations stay competitive and meet the ever-changing demands of the industrial sector.

Implementing Lean Principles in Quality Control

In today's highly competitive industrial landscape, ensuring optimal quality control processes is crucial for the success and growth of any organization. Quality control plays a vital role in meeting customer expectations, improving operational efficiency, and minimizing waste. To achieve these goals, industrial engineers are increasingly turning to the principles of Lean manufacturing.

Lean principles, originally developed by Toyota in the 1950s, focus on reducing waste, improving productivity, and enhancing customer value. By implementing Lean principles in quality control, industrial engineers can streamline processes, eliminate non-value-added activities, and promote a culture of continuous improvement. This subchapter explores the key elements and strategies of implementing Lean principles in quality control.

One of the fundamental aspects of Lean quality control is the identification and elimination of waste. Waste can take various forms, such as defects, overproduction, waiting times, excessive inventory, unnecessary processing, transportation, and motion. By analyzing the entire quality control process, industrial engineers can identify these wastes and develop strategies to eliminate or minimize them. This not only improves efficiency but also reduces costs and enhances customer satisfaction.

Another crucial aspect of Lean quality control is the concept of value stream mapping. Value stream mapping involves visually representing the entire process flow, from raw material acquisition to final product delivery. By mapping out the current state and identifying bottlenecks, delays, and redundancies, industrial engineers can identify areas for improvement and develop future-state maps that outline an ideal, more efficient process.

Furthermore, Lean quality control emphasizes the importance of employee involvement and empowerment. Industrial engineers should encourage collaboration, communication, and cross-functional teamwork among all stakeholders involved in quality control processes. This enables the identification of potential issues and the development of innovative solutions.

Continuous improvement is a core principle of Lean quality control. Industrial engineers should regularly evaluate and measure performance metrics, such as defect rates, cycle times, and customer satisfaction. By analyzing these metrics and collecting feedback from customers and employees, the quality control process can be refined and optimized further.

In conclusion, implementing Lean principles in quality control is essential for industrial engineers to achieve operational excellence and enhance customer satisfaction. By eliminating waste, mapping value streams, promoting employee involvement, and embracing continuous improvement, organizations can optimize their quality control processes and stay ahead in the dynamic industrial engineering landscape.

Sustaining Quality Control Efforts in the Long Term

In today's fast-paced and competitive industrial landscape, maintaining a high level of quality control is essential for success. Quality control is not just a one-time effort; it requires continuous monitoring, evaluation, and improvement. This subchapter explores the strategies and practices that industrial engineers can employ to sustain quality control efforts in the long term.

One of the key factors in sustaining quality control is creating a culture of quality within the organization. This starts with top management commitment and support. When leaders prioritize and emphasize the importance of quality, it filters down to every level of the organization. Employees need to understand the significance of their role in maintaining quality and be empowered to take ownership of the quality control process.

A crucial aspect of sustaining quality control efforts is the establishment of robust quality management systems (QMS). A QMS provides a framework for documenting and implementing quality control processes. It includes procedures, guidelines, and standards that ensure consistency and reliability in operations. Industrial engineers should regularly review and update the QMS to adapt to changing technologies, customer requirements, and industry trends.

Continuous improvement is at the heart of sustaining quality control efforts. Industrial engineers should encourage a culture of learning and improvement, where employees are empowered to identify and address quality issues. This can be achieved through regular training programs, workshops, and open communication channels. Collecting and analyzing data is another essential aspect of continuous improvement. Industrial engineers should utilize statistical tools and techniques to monitor and measure key quality control indicators, identify bottlenecks, and implement corrective actions.

Collaboration and partnerships are crucial for sustaining quality control efforts in the long term. Industrial engineers should work closely with suppliers, customers, and other stakeholders to ensure quality standards are met throughout the supply chain. Regular audits and certifications can also help in maintaining quality control and building trust with customers and regulatory bodies.

Lastly, technology plays a significant role in sustaining quality control efforts. Industrial engineers should leverage advanced tools such as data analytics, automation, and artificial intelligence to streamline quality control processes, reduce errors, and enhance efficiency.

In conclusion, sustaining quality control efforts in the long term is a continuous process that requires the commitment of every individual within the organization. By fostering a culture of quality, implementing robust quality management systems, promoting continuous improvement, fostering collaboration, and leveraging technology, industrial engineers can ensure that their organizations achieve and maintain the highest standards of quality control.

Chapter 8: Quality Control Case Studies

Case Study 1: Improving Product Quality in a Manufacturing Plant

Introduction:
In this subchapter, we will delve into a case study that focuses on improving product quality in a manufacturing plant. As industrial engineers, we understand the significance of maintaining high standards and delivering top-notch products to customers. This case study explores how a manufacturing plant successfully enhanced its product quality through various quality control measures, highlighting the essential role of industrial engineers in the process.

Background:
The manufacturing plant in question was facing a significant challenge in meeting customer expectations regarding product quality. Complaints and returns were on the rise, resulting in a negative impact on the company's reputation and financial performance. Recognizing the urgency, the management team decided to engage industrial engineers to analyze the existing processes, identify gaps, and propose viable solutions.

Analysis:
The industrial engineers conducted a thorough analysis of the manufacturing plant's operations, focusing on key areas such as production line efficiency, raw material quality, and employee training. They discovered that a lack of standardized processes, poor communication between departments, and outdated equipment were major contributors to the declining product quality.

Solution Implementation:
To address these issues, the industrial engineers proposed several improvements. Firstly, they introduced a comprehensive quality control system that involved regular inspections and quality checks at various stages of the production process. This ensured early detection of defects and reduced the chances of faulty products reaching customers.

Secondly, the engineers worked closely with the purchasing department to establish stringent supplier evaluation criteria. By partnering with reliable suppliers who provided superior raw materials, the plant experienced a significant improvement in product quality.

Furthermore, the engineers implemented employee training programs to enhance technical skills and foster a culture of quality consciousness. They also facilitated better communication channels between different departments, promoting coordination and collaboration to resolve any quality-related issues promptly.

Results and Conclusion:
Through the implementation of these measures, the manufacturing plant witnessed remarkable improvements in product quality. Complaints and returns drastically reduced, and customer satisfaction ratings improved significantly. The company's reputation was restored, leading to increased profitability and market share.

This case study emphasizes the critical role of industrial engineers in maintaining and improving product quality within manufacturing plants. Their expertise in analyzing processes, implementing quality control systems, and fostering a culture of excellence can make a substantial difference in achieving customer satisfaction and organizational success.

In conclusion, by investing in quality control measures and engaging industrial engineers, manufacturing plants can enhance their product quality, strengthen their market position, and build a loyal customer base. This case study serves as a valuable example for industrial engineers and professionals in the field of industrial engineering, illustrating effective strategies for mastering quality control in manufacturing plants.

Case Study 2: Enhancing Service Quality in a Healthcare Setting

Introduction:
In today's fast-paced world, the quality of healthcare services plays a crucial role in ensuring patient satisfaction and positive health outcomes. Industrial engineers are uniquely positioned to improve service quality in healthcare settings through their expertise in process optimization and quality control. This case study explores the application of industrial engineering principles to enhance service quality in a healthcare setting, showcasing the significant impact that these strategies can have on patient care.

Case Study Overview:
The case study focuses on a fictional hospital, St. Joseph's Medical Center, which has been struggling with service quality issues. Patients have reported long waiting times, inefficient processes, and poor communication, leading to frustration and decreased patient satisfaction. The industrial engineering team is tasked with identifying the root causes of these issues and implementing effective solutions to enhance service quality.

Identifying the Problem:
To begin, the team conducts a thorough analysis of the hospital's processes and collects data to identify problem areas. They observe patient flow, analyze workflow charts, and interview staff and patients to gain insights into the challenges faced. The data reveals bottlenecks, excessive paperwork, and communication gaps as the main contributors to the service quality issues.

Implementing Solutions:
Using their expertise in process optimization, the industrial engineering team devises a comprehensive plan to address the identified problems. They propose streamlining patient registration and appointment scheduling processes, implementing electronic medical records to reduce paperwork, and improving communication channels between staff and patients.

Results and Impact:
After implementing the recommended solutions, the hospital experiences a remarkable improvement in service quality. Waiting times are significantly reduced, patient registration becomes more efficient, and communication is enhanced through the use of technology. As a result, patient satisfaction scores increase, and the hospital's reputation in the community improves.

Conclusion:
This case study demonstrates the importance of industrial engineering in healthcare settings and its potential to enhance service quality. By applying their expertise in process optimization and quality control, industrial engineers can make a significant impact on patient care and satisfaction. Continuous improvement efforts in healthcare settings are essential to ensure the highest standards of service quality, ultimately leading to better patient outcomes and overall success for healthcare organizations.

Note: This content is designed to be accessible to a wide audience, including individuals from various backgrounds. The focus on industrial engineering and its application in healthcare settings caters to the niche interests of professionals in the industrial engineering field.

Case Study 3: Implementing Six Sigma in a Logistics Company

Introduction:
In today's competitive business environment, quality control has become a crucial aspect for the success of any organization. The logistics industry, in particular, requires efficient and error-free operations to ensure timely delivery of goods and services. This case study explores the implementation of Six Sigma methodology in a logistics company, highlighting the benefits and challenges faced by the organization as it embarked on this quality improvement journey.

The Need for Six Sigma in Logistics:
Logistics companies face a myriad of challenges, including complex supply chains, extensive processes, and the need for quick response times. Any errors or delays in these operations can have a significant impact on customer satisfaction and overall business performance. Recognizing this, the management of XYZ Logistics decided to adopt Six Sigma as a comprehensive quality improvement framework to tackle their operational inefficiencies.

Implementation Process:
The first step in implementing Six Sigma was to create a cross-functional team consisting of members from various departments. This team was responsible for mapping the existing processes, identifying areas of improvement, and setting specific goals. The DMAIC (Define, Measure, Analyze, Improve, Control) approach was used to guide the project.

During the Define phase, the team identified key performance indicators (KPIs) such as delivery time, order accuracy, and inventory management. The Measure phase involved collecting data from various sources to assess the current state of operations. The Analysis phase helped the team identify root causes of inefficiencies, such as inadequate training or outdated technology.

Based on the findings, improvement initiatives were implemented in the Improve phase, including process redesign, training programs, and the introduction of innovative technologies. The Control phase ensured that the improvements were sustained and monitored regularly, with appropriate metrics in place to track progress.

Benefits and Challenges:
The implementation of Six Sigma brought significant benefits to XYZ Logistics. The company experienced a drastic reduction in errors, resulting in improved customer satisfaction. Delivery times were shortened, leading to increased efficiency and a competitive edge in the market. The company also saw cost savings due to reduced waste and streamlined processes.

However, implementing Six Sigma in a logistics company was not without its challenges. Resistance to change, lack of employee engagement, and the need for extensive training were some of the hurdles faced by the organization. Overcoming these challenges required strong leadership, effective communication, and a commitment to continuous improvement.

Conclusion:
Implementing Six Sigma in a logistics company can revolutionize its operations, leading to improved efficiency, reduced costs, and increased customer satisfaction. This case study highlights the journey

of XYZ Logistics as it embraced the principles of Six Sigma and reaped the rewards. By understanding the challenges faced and the benefits obtained, industrial engineers and professionals in the field of logistics can gain valuable insights into the potential of Six Sigma in transforming their own organizations.

Case Study 4: Overcoming Quality Challenges in a Construction Project

Introduction:
In the field of industrial engineering, ensuring quality control is essential for the success of any project. This subchapter presents a case study that highlights the challenges faced in a construction project and explores the strategies employed to overcome them. By analyzing this real-life scenario, industrial engineers can gain valuable insights into quality control practices and learn effective techniques to tackle similar challenges in their own projects.

Case Study Overview:
The construction project in question involved the development of a high-rise commercial building. The project faced numerous quality challenges throughout its execution, including issues with material procurement, design changes, and coordination among various stakeholders. These challenges not only impacted the project timeline but also raised concerns about the overall quality of the final product.

Identifying the Challenges:
The first step in overcoming quality challenges is to identify them accurately. The case study outlines how the project team conducted a comprehensive assessment of the project's status to identify areas of concern. This involved analyzing documentation, conducting site visits, and engaging with project stakeholders to gain a holistic understanding of the challenges faced.

Developing a Quality Control Plan:
Once the challenges were identified, the project team formulated a

robust quality control plan. This plan focused on implementing stringent checks and balances at each stage of the project. It included quality audits, regular inspections, and documentation of quality-related processes and procedures. The case study delves into the specific steps taken to ensure the plan's successful implementation.

Mitigating Challenges:
The case study illustrates how the project team tackled each quality challenge head-on. For instance, to address material procurement issues, the team established a robust supplier management system, ensuring timely delivery of quality materials. Additionally, effective communication channels were established to manage design changes efficiently, minimizing disruptions to the project's progress. The case study also highlights the importance of collaboration among stakeholders and the measures taken to ensure seamless coordination throughout the project.

Conclusion:
This case study demonstrates how industrial engineers can overcome quality challenges in construction projects. By employing proactive measures such as comprehensive assessments, robust quality control plans, and efficient problem-solving strategies, project teams can enhance project outcomes and meet quality standards. Industrial engineers can learn from this case study to implement similar approaches in their own projects, thus contributing to the overall improvement of quality control practices in the field of industrial engineering.

Chapter 9: Future Trends and Innovations in Quality Control

Industry 4.0 and its Impact on Quality Control

In today's rapidly evolving technological landscape, Industry 4.0 has emerged as a transformative force across industries, including industrial engineering. This subchapter aims to explore the impact of Industry 4.0 on quality control and its significance for professionals in the field of industrial engineering.

Industry 4.0, also known as the Fourth Industrial Revolution, encompasses the integration of digital technologies, automation, and data exchange in manufacturing processes. It represents a paradigm shift in the way industries operate, offering immense opportunities for optimizing production, increasing efficiency, and enhancing overall quality control.

One of the key areas where Industry 4.0 has revolutionized quality control is through the application of advanced analytics and machine learning algorithms. These technologies enable the collection and analysis of vast amounts of data from various sources, such as sensors, machines, and production lines. This data-driven approach empowers industrial engineers to identify patterns, predict potential defects, and proactively address quality issues before they occur.

Additionally, the advent of smart manufacturing systems has brought about real-time monitoring and control capabilities. Industrial engineers can now track and monitor production processes in real-time, allowing for immediate identification of any deviations or abnormalities. By implementing smart sensors and Internet of Things (IoT) devices, professionals can capture crucial quality data, make informed decisions, and take corrective actions promptly.

Furthermore, the integration of robotics and automation into manufacturing processes has significantly improved quality control. Robots equipped with advanced vision systems can perform intricate inspections, ensuring high precision and consistency. This not only enhances the accuracy of quality control but also reduces human error, ultimately leading to higher product quality and customer satisfaction.

Industry 4.0 has also revolutionized supply chain management, which has a direct impact on quality control. Through technologies like blockchain and digital twins, industrial engineers can ensure traceability and transparency throughout the supply chain. This enables early identification of potential quality issues, allowing for timely interventions and improvements.

In conclusion, Industry 4.0 has brought about a paradigm shift in quality control for industrial engineers. By harnessing the power of advanced analytics, machine learning, real-time monitoring, robotics, and automation, professionals in the field can optimize production processes, enhance accuracy, and ensure higher product quality. The integration of Industry 4.0 technologies into quality control practices is crucial for industrial engineers to stay competitive and meet the ever-increasing demands of the modern manufacturing landscape.

Automation and Robotics in Quality Assurance

In today's rapidly evolving industrial landscape, the role of automation and robotics in quality assurance has become increasingly crucial. Industrial engineers, in particular, need to stay abreast of the latest advancements in this field to effectively streamline production processes and ensure consistent product quality. This subchapter aims to shed light on the various applications of automation and robotics in quality assurance, providing insights and practical guidance for industrial engineers.

Automation and robotics offer several advantages in quality assurance processes. By replacing manual labor with automated systems, manufacturers can eliminate human error, reduce variability, and enhance precision. This, in turn, leads to improved product quality and increased customer satisfaction. Moreover, automation enables continuous monitoring and real-time data analysis, allowing for timely identification and resolution of quality issues.

One key area where automation and robotics have made significant inroads is inspection and testing. Traditional manual inspection methods are time-consuming, subjective, and prone to errors. Automated inspection systems, on the other hand, use advanced sensors, cameras, and artificial intelligence algorithms to detect defects, measure dimensions, and assess product conformity with unparalleled accuracy. Industrial engineers can leverage these technologies to streamline the inspection process, reduce inspection time, and enhance the overall quality of products.

Another crucial aspect of quality assurance where automation and robotics play a vital role is in process control. Industrial engineers can employ robotics to automate repetitive tasks, such as material handling, assembly, and packaging, ensuring consistency and minimizing the risk of errors. By integrating robotics into the production line, manufacturers can achieve higher efficiency, optimize resource utilization, and maintain product quality at every stage.

Furthermore, automation and robotics also facilitate data collection and analysis, enabling engineers to monitor production parameters, identify trends, and make data-driven decisions. By harnessing the power of machine learning and artificial intelligence algorithms, industrial engineers can develop predictive models to anticipate potential quality issues and implement preventive measures proactively.

In conclusion, automation and robotics have revolutionized the field of quality assurance in industrial engineering. These technologies offer unparalleled precision, efficiency, and reliability in inspection, process control, and data analysis. Industrial engineers must embrace these advancements to master quality control and drive continuous improvement in manufacturing processes. By harnessing the potential of automation and robotics, they can enhance product quality, increase productivity, and ultimately, gain a competitive edge in today's dynamic business environment.

Artificial Intelligence and Machine Learning in Quality Control

In recent years, the field of quality control has experienced a significant transformation with the emergence of Artificial Intelligence (AI) and Machine Learning (ML) technologies. Industrial engineers, in particular, have been at the forefront of adopting these innovative tools to improve the quality and efficiency of manufacturing processes. This subchapter explores the application of AI and ML in quality control, providing a comprehensive guide for industrial engineers seeking to master these techniques.

AI and ML offer a powerful set of tools that enable industrial engineers to analyze vast amounts of data, identify patterns, and make informed decisions in real-time. By leveraging these technologies, engineers can enhance the accuracy and speed of quality control processes, resulting in improved product quality, reduced costs, and increased customer satisfaction.

One of the key applications of AI and ML in quality control is predictive analytics. By analyzing historical data, these technologies can predict potential defects or anomalies in the production process, allowing engineers to take proactive measures to prevent them. This not only minimizes waste and rework but also optimizes resource allocation.

Furthermore, AI and ML algorithms can be used to automate quality control processes. By training the algorithms on a large dataset of quality inspection results, they can learn to identify defects and anomalies with high accuracy. This eliminates the need for manual inspection, saving time and reducing human error. Additionally, these algorithms can continuously learn and adapt to new data, further improving their performance over time.

Another area where AI and ML have made significant contributions is in root cause analysis. These technologies can analyze complex datasets to identify the underlying causes of quality issues. By understanding the root causes, engineers can implement targeted solutions, leading to long-term improvements in product quality.

The subchapter also delves into the challenges and considerations when implementing AI and ML in quality control. It discusses data collection and preparation, algorithm selection, model validation, and the importance of human expertise in guiding and interpreting the results.

In conclusion, AI and ML have revolutionized the field of quality control in industrial engineering. By harnessing the power of these technologies, engineers can enhance the accuracy, efficiency, and effectiveness of quality control processes. This subchapter serves as a comprehensive guide for industrial engineers, providing the necessary knowledge and tools to master AI and ML in quality control, ultimately leading to improved product quality and customer satisfaction.

Big Data Analytics for Quality Improvement

In today's rapidly evolving digital age, the importance of quality control in industrial engineering cannot be overstated. As industries become increasingly complex and interconnected, the ability to analyze and make sense of vast amounts of data has become a crucial factor in ensuring product and process quality. This is where Big Data analytics steps in.

Big Data analytics refers to the process of examining large and diverse datasets to uncover hidden patterns, correlations, and other valuable insights. It involves harnessing advanced technologies and statistical techniques to extract meaningful information from the massive amount of data generated by various sources. By utilizing Big Data analytics, industrial engineers can gain a deeper understanding of their operations, identify areas for improvement, and make data-driven decisions to enhance quality control.

One of the primary advantages of Big Data analytics in quality improvement is its ability to identify trends and anomalies that might otherwise go unnoticed. By analyzing data from multiple sources, including production lines, supply chains, and customer feedback, industrial engineers can identify patterns that may indicate potential quality issues. This allows for proactive measures to be taken in order to prevent defects or failures before they occur, ultimately improving overall product quality.

Furthermore, Big Data analytics can help industrial engineers in optimizing their processes and reducing waste. By analyzing data collected from sensors, machines, and other devices, engineers can identify inefficiencies and bottlenecks in their production lines. This enables them to make data-driven decisions to streamline operations, minimize defects, and increase output while maintaining high quality standards.

Another significant benefit of Big Data analytics in quality improvement is its ability to facilitate predictive maintenance. By analyzing real-time data from machines and equipment, engineers can detect early signs of potential failures and take preventive actions to avoid costly breakdowns. This not only ensures uninterrupted production but also enhances product quality by reducing the likelihood of defects caused by faulty machinery.

In conclusion, Big Data analytics has emerged as a powerful tool for quality improvement in industrial engineering. By harnessing the potential of vast amounts of data, industrial engineers can gain valuable insights, optimize processes, and make informed decisions to enhance product and process quality. As industries continue to evolve, embracing Big Data analytics will be crucial for staying ahead of the competition and delivering superior products to customers.

Predictive Maintenance and Quality Control

In today's rapidly evolving industrial landscape, the need for efficient and effective quality control measures is more crucial than ever. Industrial engineering professionals play a pivotal role in ensuring that products and processes meet the highest standards of quality, thereby enhancing customer satisfaction and maximizing organizational success. One invaluable tool in this pursuit is predictive maintenance, which has emerged as a game-changer in the field of quality control.

Predictive maintenance is a proactive approach to maintenance that utilizes advanced data analytics and machine learning algorithms to predict equipment failures and schedule maintenance activities accordingly. By continuously monitoring and analyzing real-time data from sensors and other sources, industrial engineers can identify potential issues before they occur, allowing them to take preventive action. This approach not only minimizes downtime and production losses but also enhances product quality by reducing the likelihood of defects caused by faulty machinery.

The integration of predictive maintenance into quality control processes offers several advantages. First and foremost, it enables industrial engineers to transition from a reactive to a proactive maintenance strategy. Instead of waiting for equipment failures to happen and then scrambling to fix them, engineers can now anticipate and address potential issues in advance. This not only saves time and resources but also prevents disruptions in production, ensuring a smooth workflow and consistent product quality.

Moreover, predictive maintenance allows for the optimization of maintenance schedules. By accurately predicting when equipment is likely to fail, engineers can schedule maintenance activities during planned downtime, avoiding costly unplanned shutdowns. This approach ensures that equipment is kept in optimal working condition, reducing the risk of defects and ensuring product quality remains uncompromised.

Furthermore, predictive maintenance facilitates the collection and analysis of vast amounts of data. By leveraging data analytics tools, industrial engineers can identify patterns and trends, gaining valuable insights into the root causes of quality issues. This knowledge can then be used to refine processes, improve product designs, and enhance overall quality control strategies.

In conclusion, the incorporation of predictive maintenance into quality control practices is a game-changer for industrial engineering professionals. By embracing this proactive approach, engineers can enhance product quality, minimize downtime, and optimize maintenance schedules. As the industrial landscape continues to evolve, mastering predictive maintenance is essential for industrial engineers to stay ahead and ensure that their organizations remain competitive in today's quality-driven market.

Chapter 10: Conclusion and Final Thoughts

Recap of Key Concepts and Strategies

In this subchapter, we will revisit the essential concepts and strategies covered in the book "Mastering Quality Control: A Guide for Industrial Engineers." Whether you are a seasoned industrial engineer or just starting in the field, this recap will serve as a valuable refresher and reference guide.

Key Concepts:

1. Quality Control: Quality control is the systematic process of ensuring that products or services meet or exceed customer expectations. It involves the identification, measurement, and correction of deviations from the desired quality standards.

2. Statistical Process Control (SPC): SPC is a statistical tool used to monitor and control processes. It provides a proactive approach to quality control by using statistical methods to analyze data and detect variations in real-time, allowing for timely corrective actions.

3. Six Sigma: Six Sigma is a data-driven approach aimed at reducing defects and variation in processes. It emphasizes the importance of improving process capability and achieving near-perfect quality levels by minimizing variability.

4. Total Quality Management (TQM): TQM is a management philosophy that focuses on continuous improvement and customer satisfaction. It involves the active involvement of all employees in

quality improvement efforts, fostering a culture of quality throughout the organization.

Key Strategies:

1. Plan-Do-Check-Act (PDCA) Cycle: The PDCA cycle, also known as the Deming cycle, is a four-step iterative process for continuous improvement. It involves planning, executing, evaluating, and making necessary adjustments to achieve desired quality outcomes.

2. Root Cause Analysis (RCA): RCA is a problem-solving technique used to identify the underlying causes of quality issues. By addressing the root cause, rather than just the symptoms, engineers can develop effective solutions and prevent recurrence.

3. Design of Experiments (DOE): DOE is a systematic method for investigating and optimizing processes and product designs. It allows engineers to identify the key factors affecting quality and determine the optimal settings to achieve desired outcomes.

4. Failure Modes and Effects Analysis (FMEA): FMEA is a proactive risk assessment tool used to identify and prioritize potential failure modes in a process or product. By understanding the potential impact and likelihood of failures, engineers can take preventive measures to mitigate risks.

By revisiting and reinforcing these key concepts and strategies, you will be equipped with the knowledge and tools necessary to excel in the field of industrial engineering. Remember, quality control is a continuous journey, and mastering it requires a commitment to lifelong learning and improvement.

Importance of Continuous Learning and Adaptation in Quality Control

In the fast-paced world of industrial engineering, quality control plays a vital role in ensuring that products and services meet the highest standards. However, the field of quality control is constantly evolving, and what worked yesterday may not work today. This is why continuous learning and adaptation are of utmost importance in the realm of quality control.

Continuous learning is the process of acquiring new knowledge, skills, and techniques to stay updated with the latest developments in the field. As an industrial engineer, it is crucial to keep up with emerging trends, technologies, and best practices in quality control. This allows you to make informed decisions, implement effective quality control procedures, and improve overall product quality.

Adaptation, on the other hand, involves adjusting your quality control processes to meet changing circumstances. Whether it's new regulations, customer demands, or advancements in technology, being able to adapt is essential for maintaining high-quality standards. By continuously learning and adapting, you can ensure that your quality control processes remain relevant and effective.

One of the key benefits of continuous learning and adaptation in quality control is improved efficiency. As you gain new knowledge and skills, you become more proficient in identifying potential quality issues and implementing preventive measures. This helps you catch defects early on, saving time and resources in the long run.

Continuous learning and adaptation also contribute to enhanced customer satisfaction. By staying up-to-date with the latest quality control practices, you can address customer concerns more effectively and deliver products that meet or exceed their expectations. This not only helps build trust and loyalty but also gives you a competitive edge in the market.

Moreover, continuous learning and adaptation foster a culture of innovation within your organization. As you explore new quality control methods and technologies, you may discover more efficient and cost-effective ways of ensuring product quality. This can lead to process improvements, increased productivity, and ultimately, higher profitability.

In summary, continuous learning and adaptation are essential for industrial engineers involved in quality control. By staying updated with industry trends and adjusting your processes accordingly, you can improve efficiency, enhance customer satisfaction, and drive innovation. Embracing a mindset of continuous learning and adaptation will not only benefit your organization but also contribute to the overall advancement of the field of industrial engineering.

Final Words of Encouragement for Industrial Engineers on Mastering Quality Control

Congratulations on taking the first step towards mastering quality control as an industrial engineer! As you near the end of this comprehensive guide, it is important to reflect on your journey and gather the final words of encouragement that will propel you towards success in the field of industrial engineering.

Quality control is a crucial aspect of any industrial engineering process, as it directly impacts the overall efficiency and effectiveness of operations. By mastering quality control techniques, you will not only enhance your own professional reputation but also contribute to the growth and success of the industries you serve.

Throughout this book, you have gained valuable insights into various quality control methodologies, statistical tools, and process improvement techniques. From understanding the fundamentals of quality control to implementing Six Sigma methodologies, you now possess a solid foundation to tackle real-world quality challenges.

However, knowledge alone is not enough. To become a true master of quality control, you must apply what you have learned. Embrace every opportunity to practice and refine your skills in a real-world setting. Seek out internships, projects, or collaborations with professionals in the field to gain hands-on experience. Remember, it is through practical application that your understanding of quality control will truly deepen.

As an industrial engineer, it is essential to be proactive in staying updated with the latest advancements and trends in quality control.

The field is constantly evolving, and new tools and techniques emerge regularly. Attend conferences, workshops, and webinars to network with experts and learn from their experiences. Engage in continuous learning to ensure that your knowledge remains relevant and up to date.

Lastly, never underestimate the power of collaboration. Quality control is a multidisciplinary field, and working alongside professionals from different niches can expand your horizons and offer fresh perspectives. Collaborate with colleagues, share your ideas, and actively seek feedback. The collective intelligence and diverse backgrounds of your peers can fuel your growth and help you overcome challenges more effectively.

In conclusion, mastering quality control as an industrial engineer requires a combination of knowledge, practical application, continuous learning, and collaboration. The journey may not always be easy, but by persevering and applying the principles outlined in this book, you have the potential to become a leader in the field of industrial engineering. Embrace the challenge, stay curious, and never stop striving for excellence. Best of luck on your journey to mastering quality control!

www.ingramcontent.com/pod-product-compliance
Lightning Source LLC
LaVergne TN
LVHW020450070526
838199LV00063B/4898